VEGETABL...

GROW THEM, COOK THEM, EAT THEM

Charlotte Popescu

CAVALIER PAPERBACKS

Published by Cavalier Paperbacks 2004

Cavalier Paperbacks
Burnham House,
Upavon,
Wilts SN9 6DU

www.cavalierpaperbacks.co.uk

ISBN 1-899470-25-5

Printed and bound in Great Britain by Cromwell Press, White Horse Business Park, Trowbridge, Wilts

CONTENTS

Asparagus	5
Aubergine	10
Beetroot	14
Broad Beans	20
Broccoli	24
Brussels Sprouts	32
Cabbage	37
Carrots	43
Cauliflower	54
Celery and Celeriac	62
Chicory, Endive and Radicchio	66
Courgettes and Marrows	72
Cucumber	82
Florence Fennel	86
French Beans and Runner Beans	89
Jerusalem Artichoke	96
Kale	100
Leek	104
Lettuce and Rocket	110
Onion	116
Parsnip	122
Peas and Mangetout	129
Peppers	139
Potato	144
Pumpkin and Squash	153
Radish	161
Spinach and Chard	164
Sweetcorn	176
Tomato	181
Turnip and Swede	186
My Gardening Calendar	188
Index	189

INTRODUCTION

This book should be useful to those of you thinking of growing vegetables or those who want to expand their vegetable gardens and aim to be a little more self-sufficient. It is based mostly on personal experience although there are several vegetables included that I have not grown. The recipes will, I hope, be helpful for those with a sudden glut of one particular vegetable and will give you some ideas for cooking or preparing them. I have arranged the vegetables in alphabetical order for easy reference. I enjoy growing a variety of vegetables so that there is always something available to harvest even in the winter and early spring. My children also help with planting and harvesting their favourite vegetables which include mangetout, purple sprouting broccoli and the many varieties of salad leaves we grow - they especially like the red-leaved cut-and-come-again salads and the Giant Mustard leaves. Radishes and runner beans are also easy for younger members of the family to grow and digging up the potatoes can be fun.

I have covered what I consider to be 40 of the most popular vegetables for growing but not the more unusual sorts such as kohlrabi, cardoon, okra, salsify or globe artichokes partly due to limitations on space. I order seeds by mail order and recommend Suffolk Herbs, Edwin Tucker & Sons and Simpson's Seeds.

In all cases when cooking vegetables the best way is to steam them. Steaming means only 6.3% nutrients are lost, in contrast to boiling in which 64% are lost and if you cook your vegetables in the microwave a massive 86% of nutrients are lost. Most home grown vegetables should be eaten, whether raw or cooked, as soon after harvesting them as you can because they can start losing precious nutrients straightaway.

I keep bantams so it is very satisfying being able to produce a whole meal from the garden - an omelette with herbs, potatoes and a wonderful salad or some mangetout or beans.

Finally a number of recipes need vegetable stock and I always use Marigold Swiss Vegetable Bouillon Powder.

ASPARAGUS

Asparagus is a perennial, a member of the lily family and one of the oldest cultivated vegetables. It was first eaten by the ancient Egyptians and Greeks. There is a Greek legend that asparagus grew from a ram's horn stuck in the ground. The word asparagus is Greek and means sprout or shoot. The Romans also grew and enjoyed asparagus. The Emperor Augustus coined the phrase 'velocius quam asparagi conquantur' meaning to do something faster than you can cook asparagus. Caesar liked to serve it with butter. The Romans introduced asparagus to Britain but after they left it was not re-introduced until the 1500s and then it came from France. It was known as sparrow grass and that is how Samuel Pepys referred to it. In the time of King Louis XIV it was known as 'The King of Vegetables' and he had special greenhouses built so that he could eat asparagus all year round.

You may think twice about introducing it into your vegetable patch though as you have to wait three years before cutting your first spears. You may prefer to buy it from your local farm shop where it is available from May to the end of June. It is best eaten as soon after it has been picked as possible.

If you do decide to grow your own asparagus it is best to buy one year old crowns. Two and three year old crowns may be available and it is tempting to go for these as you won't have to wait so long but they don't transplant well. Asparagus likes a sandy soil which has been well manured the previous autumn. Planting is best done towards the end of March and the bed should be completely free of perennial weeds. Allow about 60cm, 2ft between the crowns. Planting is quite tricky. You should dig out a 22cm, 9in trench and spread out the spider-like roots on a slight mound at the bottom of the trench. Cover the roots with soil and make sure the crowns are about 12cm, 5in below the bed level. The shoots will begin to appear from mid May but you must not cut them. Instead the shoots must be left to make fern (foliage) which dies back in the autumn to provide the roots with the nourishment they need to build up into a robust plant. There is not much to do over the next two years except keep the bed weed free. In the third year when you can cut the spears, remove only two per plant allowing the rest to make foliage. The next year you can cut the shoots from about mid May until the end of June.

The advantage of growing asparagus is that the crowns should last for twenty years. Asparagus is a nutritious vegetable and is high in folic acid. It is a good source of potassium, Vitamin B6, A and C. A versatile vegetable which can be used to make soup, in flans and risotto or with pasta, asparagus goes well with eggs or cheese. Do not, however, drink red wine with asparagus because apparently the sulphur in asparagus can make the wine taste metallic.

ASPARAGUS CREAM SOUP
Serves 2 - 3

450g, 1lb asparagus
600ml, 1pt stock from cooking the asparagus
25g, 1oz butter
25g, 1oz flour
1 onion, peeled and chopped
1 tsp lemon juice
a pinch of sugar
4 tbsp single cream

Cook the asparagus in boiling water for 10 minutes. Reserve the liquid and use this to make up your stock. Melt the butter in a large saucepan and stir in the flour, gradually adding the stock. Cut the tips off the asparagus and reserve them. Chop up the rest of the asparagus and add to the sauce with the onion. Cover and simmer for 20 minutes. Liquidize the mixture and return to the pan. Stir in the lemon juice, sugar and cream. Bring just to the boil, add the asparagus tips and serve at once.

CHAR GRILLED ASPARAGUS WITH BREADCRUMB TOPPING
Serves 3 – 4

450g, 1lb asparagus spears, washed and trimmed
a little olive oil
25g, 1oz butter
50g, 2oz brown breadcrumbs
1 tbsp fresh parsley, chopped
2 boiled egg yolks, mashed
salt and pepper
50g, 2oz butter, melted (optional)

Brush your griddle pan with a little olive oil. Char grill the asparagus until just tender. In the meantime melt the butter in a frying pan, add the breadcrumbs and fry until brown. Remove from the heat and add the parsley and egg yolk. Season with salt and pepper. Arrange the asparagus on a plate and sprinkle the topping over them. Serve with a little melted butter if liked.

CREAMED CHICKEN WITH ASPARAGUS
Serves 4

225g, 8oz asparagus spears, washed and trimmed
300ml, ½pt white sauce
350g, 12oz cooked chicken, diced
50g, 2oz brown breadcrumbs
50g, 2oz mature Cheddar cheese, grated
25g, 1oz butter

Steam the asparagus. Stir the chicken into the white sauce and pour into a greased ovenproof dish. Arrange the asparagus spears over the chicken and top with breadcrumbs and cheese. Dot with the butter. Bake in the oven at gas mark 5, 190°C (375°F) for 15 to 20 minutes.

ASPARAGUS WITH CREAM CHEESE
Serves 6

450g, 1lb asparagus spears, trimmed
100g, 4oz cream cheese
2 egg yolks
1 tsp lemon juice
6 slices of Ciabatta bread, toasted
6 slices of ham

Cook the asparagus preferably by steaming it until just tender. Beat up the cream cheese with the egg yolks and mix in the lemon juice. Place the bowl over a pan of simmering water and stir until the cheese mixture is hot. Arrange a slice of ham over each piece of toast and top with some asparagus spears. Pour the cheese sauce over the asparagus and serve at once.

ASPARAGUS AND BROAD BEAN RISOTTO
Serves 4

225g, 8oz asparagus spears, trimmed
175g, 6oz broad beans
1 onion, peeled and chopped
15g, ½oz butter
2 tbsp olive oil
225g, 8oz arborio rice
900ml, 1½pts vegetable stock
150ml, ¼pt dry white wine
50g, 2oz Parmesan, grated
Salt, pepper and a little extra butter
1 tbsp fresh basil, chopped

Cut the asparagus into 5cm, 2in lengths and steam for a couple of minutes. Cook the broad beans in salted, boiling water until just tender. Melt the butter and oil in a large frying pan and add the onion. When the onion has softened add the rice and stir it around to coat with the oil. Then gradually add the stock, a spoonful at a time. Allow the liquid to be absorbed before you add any more. Add the wine a little at a time. The risotto should be just about cooked after 15 minutes. Before you add the last spoonful of liquid add the asparagus and broad beans and stir them in. Lastly add the Parmesan, the seasoning and a little extra butter.

ASPARAGUS AND RED ONION FLAN
Serves 5 – 6

225g, 8oz shortcrust pastry
175g, 6oz asparagus spears
4 rashers streaky unsmoked bacon
1 red onion, peeled and sliced
1 tbsp olive oil
2 eggs
90ml, 3fl oz milk
90ml, 3fl oz single cream
50g, 2oz mature Cheddar cheese, grated

Roll out the pastry and use to line a greased 20cm, 8in flan tin. Bake blind at gas mark 5, 190°C (375°F) for 15 minutes. Meanwhile trim the asparagus of any woody stems and steam for 5 minutes. Chop up the bacon and fry in a dry frying pan for several minutes. Add the onion and oil and fry for several more minutes. Mix in the asparagus. Scatter the bacon, onion and asparagus evenly over the pastry base. Beat together the eggs, milk and cream and pour over the asparagus mixture. Sprinkle over the grated cheese and cook in the oven for a further 20 to 25 minutes until the filling is golden brown.

AUBERGINE

Aubergines were grown in China around 400BC and were popular in ancient times in India. They were unknown to the Greeks and Romans. They were called 'apples of love' by sixteenth century Spaniards and arrived in Britain from Spain at about this time. The Americans refer to them as egg-plants (there is a white variety which looks like a goose egg).

They are essentially a greenhouse crop although you may be lucky and be able to finish them off out of doors in a good summer. For greenhouse plants sow seeds in early February in pots using a seed compost. Keep at a temperature of 60°F (16°C). Seeds may take two weeks to germinate. Move the seedlings to larger pots and when the plants are 15cm, 6in high, pinch out the growing tips. Allow only four fruits to set per plant – remove the rest of the flowers and pinch out all the side shoots. You should be picking your aubergines from August onwards.

Aubergines contain an insignificant amount of vitamins and minerals. However they contain flavonoids, the cancer fighting antioxidants and are known to have antibacterial and diuretic effects. Aubergines are low in calories until you add oil which they absorb in substantial quantities when you fry them.

AUBERGINE DIP
Serves 4 – 6

2 aubergines
1 onion, peeled and grated
2 tbsp lemon juice
2 cloves of garlic, peeled and crushed
120ml, 4fl oz olive oil
2 tbsp fresh parsley, chopped

Grill the aubergines, turning frequently until the skins are black and blistered. Hold under running water and peel off the skins. Halve the aubergines and scoop out the flesh. Mash it along with the onion, lemon juice and garlic. Add the olive oil a little at a time and beat in a tablespoon of the parsley. Turn into a serving bowl and sprinkle with the rest of the parsley. Serve with Pitta bread.

RATATOUILLE
Serves 4

3 tbsp olive oil
1 onion, peeled and chopped
1 aubergine, diced
2 courgettes, sliced
1 red pepper, deseeded and chopped
1 clove of garlic, peeled and crushed
400g, 14oz tin of tomatoes
salt and pepper
1 tsp mixed herbs

Heat the oil in a large saucepan and fry the onion, aubergine and courgettes. Add the pepper, garlic, tomatoes, seasoning and herbs. Cover and simmer for about 30 minutes, adding a little water if the mixture becomes too dry.

MOUSSAKA
Serves 6

2 tbsp olive oil
450g, 1lb cooked lamb, left over from a joint and diced
1 onion, peeled and chopped
1 tbsp soya sauce
4 large potatoes, peeled and par-boiled
1 aubergine, sliced
extra olive oil
400g, 14oz tin of tomatoes
1 clove of garlic, peeled and chopped

Topping

25g, 1oz margarine
25g, 1oz flour
300ml, ½pt milk
100g, 4oz mature Cheddar cheese, grated

Fry the lamb and onion in the oil until browned. Transfer to an ovenproof dish and sprinkle with soya sauce. Slice the potatoes and fry in the same pan adding a little extra oil if necessary. Use a slotted spoon to take them out and arrange on top of the meat. Now fry the aubergine slices using some extra oil and when most of the slices are nicely browned, tip in the tomatoes and add the garlic. Continue to cook over a gentle heat for a few more minutes and then spread on top of the potatoes. To make the sauce, melt the margarine in a small saucepan, stir in the flour and gradually add the milk. Pour the sauce over the aubergine mixture and scatter the cheese over the top. Bake in the oven at gas mark 5, 190°C (375°F) for 30 minutes or until golden and bubbling on top.

AUBERGINES PARMIGIANA
Serves 3 – 4

2 aubergines, sliced lengthways
4 tbsp olive oil
1 onion, peeled and chopped
400g, 14oz tin of tomatoes
1 tbsp tomato purée
clove of garlic, peeled and chopped
1 tbsp fresh basil, chopped
pinch of sugar
salt and pepper to taste
225g, 8oz mozzarella
50g, 2oz Parmesan, grated

Fry the aubergine slices in some of the olive oil and drain on paper towels. Heat the rest of the olive oil in a large saucepan and fry the onion. Add the tin of tomatoes, tomato purée, garlic and basil. Add the sugar, salt and pepper to taste. Allow to simmer for a few minutes. Spoon some of the tomato mixture into an ovenproof dish and lay some of the aubergine slices on top and then a layer of mozzarella. Continue the layers in this way and finish with some mozzarella. Sprinkle the Parmesan on top. Bake in the oven at gas mark 5, 190°C (375°F) for 20 minutes until the cheese is bubbling and lightly browned.

BEETROOT

Beetroot as we know it today was developed by German gardeners in the Middle Ages. The Romans grew beetroot but used it for its young leaves, only realising about the value of the swollen root later on. Beetroot has only really been popular in Britain since Tudor times. There are four types of beet: beetroot; spinach beet or chard; sugar beet (developed by Napoleon and now commercially a very important crop) and mangel-wurzel (used for cattle fodder). Beetroot grows best in cooler regions which is why some of the best recipes come from Northern Europe and Russia in particular.

Beetroot is relatively easy to grow and you can use the leaves just like spinach as well as the root. There are various types and shapes that you can grow. Of the globe or round shapes, Boltardy is probably one of the best to grow as it is an early cropper and is resistant to bolting. There are also tapered varieties and there is Barbabietola di Chioggia, an Italian type that has unusual white rings when sliced.

Seeds can be planted under cloches in March for early harvesting in July. The main crop should be sown between May and July. Sow in drills about 2cm, ¾in deep and thin to a final spacing of 7.5cm, 3in apart. Seeds are actually a cluster so several plants develop from one seed – you will therefore need to thin them out to a single plant when they are about 2.5cm, 1in high. Plants need an even supply of water – too much and they may split and too little and they get woody. In very dry weather water every two weeks. Beetroot takes 60 – 90 days to mature and normal globe shaped beetroots are mature when the size of a cricket ball. One pest that you might encounter when growing beetroot is the flea beetle which attacks the leaves, making holes and preventing you from using the leaves in salads. Otherwise they are usually pest free.

Beetroots must be handled carefully before cooking as, if you pierce the skin at all, the beet will bleed. Twist off the leaves carefully and don't cut off the ends! The red colour comes from the cell sap but varieties in other colours such as yellow and pink have been developed. Cook them in boiling salted water for about 45 minutes or you can bake them whole for about an hour. Peel them using plastic gloves otherwise you will stain your hands red.

Beetroot is higher in carbohydrates than most vegetables and is a good source of folic acid and potassium. It also has a high natural sugar content which is why it can be used successfully in some cake recipes. It is particularly high in folate, a B vitamin which is necessary for normal tissue growth. The red pigmentation, betacyanin, contains anti-cancer agents. Beetroot's potential effectiveness against colon cancer has been demonstrated in several studies. The leafy tops are a good source of calcium, iron and beta-carotene.

HOT BORSCHT SOUP
Serves 6 – 8

4 large beetroot
1 onion, peeled and sliced
2 cloves of garlic, peeled and crushed
juice of 1 lemon
3 litres, 5pts water
450g, 1lb potatoes, peeled and diced
1 tbsp white wine vinegar
1 tbsp sugar
pinch of salt

Cut the spinach-like tops off each beetroot and chop them up. Peel the beetroots and grate them, using plastic gloves. Put in a large saucepan with the onion, garlic, lemon and water. Cover and bring to the boil, then turn down the heat and simmer for 25 minutes. Add the potatoes, vinegar, and beetroot tops. Cook for another 10 minutes, adding the sugar and some salt to taste.

BEETROOT AND TOMATO SOUP
Serves 4 - see photo in colour section

25g, 1oz butter
225g, 8oz raw beetroot, peeled and grated
1 onion, peeled and chopped
1 tsp ground cumin
pinch of cinnamon
pinch of cloves
900ml, 1½pts vegetable stock
400g, 14oz tin of tomatoes + 1 tbsp tomato purée
2 tbsp Greek yoghurt + fresh herbs for garnish

Melt the butter in a large saucepan and sauté the beetroot and onion. Add spices and cook for a couple of minutes. Add the stock, tomatoes and purée, cover and simmer for 30 minutes, stirring every so often. Purée in a blender or processor until smooth. Reheat gently and spoon into bowls adding a dollop of yoghurt and a sprinkling of herbs to each portion.

BEETROOT BAKED IN CREAM AND LEMON
Serves 6 as a side dish

900g, 2lb cooked beetroot
grated rind of 1 lemon
150ml, ¼pt single cream
salt and pepper
2 tbsp breadcrumbs
1 tbsp fresh dill, chopped

Butter a shallow ovenproof dish. Slice the beetroot and arrange the slices in the dish. Sprinkle the lemon rind over the beetroot. Pour over the cream and season. Bake in the oven at gas mark 4, 180°C (350°F) for 20 minutes. Sprinkle over the breadcrumbs and put under a hot grill to finish off. Sprinkle the dill over the breadcrumbs and serve.

BEETROOT, SPINACH AND MACKEREL SALAD
Serves 4 - see photo in colour section

100g, 4oz young spinach leaves
225g, 8oz smoked mackerel, skinned and flaked
2 cooked beetroot, cut into rounds
4 tbsp fromage frais
1 tbsp lemon juice
1 tsp creamed horseradish

Spread the spinach leaves on a serving dish and scatter the mackerel on top. Arrange the beetroot over the mackerel. Mix together the fromage frais, lemon juice and horseradish and pour evenly over the salad.

BEETROOT AND TUNA QUICHE
Serves 4 – 6

225g, 8oz shortcrust pastry
1 red onion, peeled and chopped
25g, 1oz butter
175g, 6oz cooked beetroot, diced
175g, 6oz new potatoes, cooked and diced
185g, 7oz tin of tuna, drained
150ml, ¼pt soured cream
150ml, ¼pt milk
2 eggs, beaten
100g, 4oz mature Cheddar cheese, grated

Roll out the pastry and use to line a greased 20cm, 8in flan tin. Bake blind in the oven at gas mark 4, 180°C (350°F) for 10 minutes. Fry the onion in the butter, and stir in the beetroot and potato. Scatter evenly over the pastry base along with the tuna. Beat the soured cream, milk and eggs together. Pour over the beetroot mixture and scatter the cheese over the top. Return to the oven for about 20 minutes or until set and golden.

BEETROOT AND CHOCOLATE CAKE
Serves 8

This cake is delicious – the flavour of the beetroot comes through if you keep the cake for a couple of days.

225g, 8oz self-raising flour
1 tsp baking powder
25g, 1oz cocoa powder
100g, 4oz raw beetroot, peeled
100g, 4oz golden caster sugar
1 tsp vanilla essence
2 eggs, beaten
75g, 3oz plain chocolate
75g, 3oz butter

Filling

50g, 2oz butter
100g, 4oz icing sugar
1 tsp lemon juice
½ tsp lemon zest

Sift together the flour, baking powder and cocoa powder. Grate the beetroot using plastic gloves to avoid staining your hands red. Stir the sugar, grated beetroot, vanilla essence and beaten eggs into the dry ingredients. Melt the butter and chocolate together in a microwave or over a gentle heat and stir to combine before adding to the cake mixture. Spoon into 2 greased 17.5cm, 7in cake tins and bake in the oven at gas mark 4, 180°C (350°F) for 35 minutes or until a skewer in the cakes comes out clean. To make the filling beat the icing sugar into the butter and add the lemon juice and zest. Sandwich the cakes together and sift a little icing sugar over the cake before serving.

BEETROOT SALAD
Serves 4 - 6

3 cooked beetroot, sliced
1 tbsp olive oil
3 tbsp white wine vinegar
1 tbsp granulated sugar
1 clove of garlic, peeled and crushed
seasoning of salt and pepper

Mix together the dressing ingredients and pour over the beetroot. Leave for several hours, turning over the beetroot in the marinade every so often. Most of the liquid will be absorbed but this produces delicious-tasting beetroot.

BEETROOT RELISH
Makes about 700g, 1½lb

900g, 2lb beetroot, cooked, skinned and diced
450g, 1lb white cabbage, chopped
75g, 3oz fresh horseradish, grated
1 tbsp mustard powder
600ml, 1pt malt vinegar
225g, 8oz granulated sugar
pinch of cayenne pepper
sprinkling of salt and pepper

Combine all the ingredients in a large saucepan. Bring slowly to the boil and then simmer for 30 minutes, stirring every so often. Spoon into sterilised jars and seal. Leave to mature for at least 2 months before eating if you can.

BROAD BEANS

Broad beans have been around for thousands of years. They are thought to have originated around the Mediterranean, the oldest remains of beans being dated to about 6500BC. In the first century AD Dioscorides described them in his Greek Herbal as 'flatulent, hard of digestion and causing troublesome dreams'. The Romans introduced them into Britain. They were grown in the past by poor people as they are particularly rich in protein and were sustaining during a hard day's work.

Broad beans bridge the gap in the garden between spring greens and purple sprouting broccoli and the first of the summer crops. They like a deeply worked soil and preferably one that has been manured for a previous crop. They can be planted in November (recommended varieties are Super Aquadulce or Aquadulce Claudia) and this will ensure an early crop. Otherwise they can be sown in pots and kept in a cold frame in January for planting out in March or in the South of England you can plant seeds out in February.

Broad beans make attractive plants in the vegetable garden with their black-spotted white flowers which are particularly attractive to bees. However they can be badly affected by black bean aphids. These black flies can stunt growth, damage flowers and ruin the pods. If you pinch off the top 7.5cm, 3in of stem of each plant when the pods first begin to form this may help control the aphids. Planting summer savory alongside the broad bean plants can also discourage them. Do not water until the flowers appear and then water at the base of the plant.

Pick pods when the beans begin to show – if picked very young the pods can be eaten whole – leave the pods to become too large and the beans inside will be tough.

Broad beans are highly nutritious containing vitamins A and C, and are an excellent source of phosphorus. They are used extensively in Middle Eastern dishes and are the national dish of

Egypt – an old Arab saying goes, 'Beans have satisfied even the Pharaohs'.

Broad beans work very well with savory and if possible try and add a sprig to the water when cooking your beans as it brings out the flavour. Broad beans freeze very well – just wash and blanch in boiling water for 3 minutes.

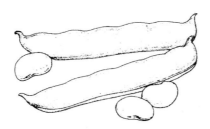

BROAD BEAN AND MINT SOUP
Serves 3 – 4

1 tbsp sunflower oil
1 onion, peeled and chopped
1 clove of garlic, peeled and crushed
2 potatoes, peeled and chopped
300ml, ½pt vegetable stock
450g, 1lb broad beans, shelled
juice of 1 lemon
300ml, ½pt single cream
1 sprig of mint

Heat the oil in a large pan and add the onions and garlic. Cook until they soften, then add the potato and stock. Simmer for 20 minutes. Meanwhile cook the broad beans in boiling water for 5 minutes and then add them to the stock and potato. Leave to cool and then add the lemon juice, cream and mint. Purée, reheat and serve.

BROAD BEAN AND HAM SALAD
Serves 2 – 3

225g, 8oz broad beans, shelled
3 tbsp olive oil
1 tbsp balsamic vinegar
1 tbsp fresh parsley, chopped
¼ tsp dry mustard
pinch of salt and pepper
100g, 4oz cooked ham, sliced
2 hard-boiled eggs, chopped

Bring some water in a saucepan to the boil and add the broad beans. Simmer for 5 minutes. Whisk together the oil, vinegar, parsley, mustard, salt and pepper. Drain the beans and mix in the dressing while they are still warm. Allow to cool and stir in the ham and egg.

BROAD BEANS WITH CREAM AND BACON
Serves 6

675g, 1½lb broad beans, shelled
a sprig of savory
6 rashers unsmoked streaky bacon, chopped
25g, 1oz butter
3 tbsp double cream
2 tbsp fresh chives, chopped

Cook the broad beans in boiling water with the savory added for 5 minutes. Drain and slip the skins off unless the beans are very young. Fry the bacon in a little of the butter and then add the rest along with the beans. Stir in the cream and scatter the chives over the beans just before serving.

CREAMY BROAD BEANS WITH SWEETCORN
Serves 4 as a side vegetable

225g, 8oz broad beans, shelled
175g, 6oz sweetcorn
25g, 1oz butter
120ml, 4fl oz double cream
1 tsp fresh parsley, chopped

Cook the broad beans in boiling water for 5 minutes. Heat the sweetcorn through in a saucepan with a little water and the butter. Drain and stir in the cream. Remove the skins from the broad beans and stir them in with the parsley.

BROAD BEAN OMELETTE
Serves 3 – 4

225g, 8oz broad beans, shelled
3 rashers of bacon, chopped
2 tbsp single cream
1 tbsp olive oil
4 eggs
1 tbsp fresh parsley, chopped

Cook the broad beans in boiling water for 5 minutes. Drain and skin. Dry fry the bacon until crisp. Stir together the beans, bacon and the cream. In the meantime beat the eggs together and after heating the oil in a large frying pan, pour in the egg mixture. Fry until the omelette is cooked on the underside. Spoon the bean and bacon mixture into the centre before folding the omelette over. Keep over a low heat for a couple more minutes, scatter with parsley and serve immediately.

BROCCOLI

Broccoli is an Italian word, derived from the Latin brachium, meaning branch or arm and indeed broccoli does look similar to the large branch of a tree. It therefore seems pretty likely that broccoli originated in Italy and was probably developed from the cabbage plant, possibly by the Etruscans who were around about 1100BC. The Romans conquered Etruria, today's Tuscany, in 200BC and Apicius, the famous Roman cookery writer, used it in his recipes. Pliny also mentioned that Tiberius enjoyed broccoli. The historical record is sparse and we know very little about the growing of broccoli between the time of the Roman empire until the 16th century. At that time we learn that Catherine de Medici, on marrying Henry II, King of France, moved to Paris from her native Tuscany bringing vegetables with her, including broccoli, green beans, peas, artichokes and cabbage. Broccoli spread from Italy and France to Northern Europe and arrived in Britain in the eighteenth century. At that time it seemed to be known as Italian Asparagus. Calabrese, a similar plant, originated in Calabria and was introduced to France before spreading to the rest of Europe.

Purple sprouting broccoli is probably the most popular variety for home growing. It is hardy and produces a succession of small flowerheads for cropping over a long season from winter to late spring, a time when not many other vegetables are in season.

You can either grow broccoli from seeds in a propagator or greenhouse or buy plants to plant out in May. You should leave about 60cm, 2ft between plants and between rows. They do take up a lot of space, grow quite tall and have a long growing season so be warned! In my experience the seedlings tend to grow with slightly crooked stems. You will probably have a problem with caterpillars eating the leaves as the broccoli plants develop. You should pick them off by hand. Do not get too disheartened – the lower leaves tend to shrivel and can be picked off and the broccoli seems to develop successfully despite the caterpillars. The plants tend to be top heavy so you can either earth them up or stake them to prevent them toppling over. Harvest the heads before they have a chance to flower. If you harvest regularly without stripping each plant completely, the side shoots will keep providing more heads so you should be able to pick broccoli over a period of about eight weeks. Calabrese is grown in the same way but produces a large central flowerhead. Once harvested the plant will produce smaller sideshoots. Broccoletto is a quick maturing variety that I am trying.

Broccoli is a highly nutritious vegetable containing vitamins A and C and is an excellent source of calcium, and a good source for potassium and iron. It is also loaded with phytochemicals such as beta-carotene, indoles, isothiocyanates and glucosinolates which break down into sulforaphane, a compound with an antibiotic and anti-cancer effect.

CHEESY BROCCOLI SOUP
Serves 4

25g, 1oz butter
1 onion, peeled and chopped
1 large potato, peeled
450g, 1lb broccoli
600ml, 1pt vegetable stock
sprinkling of salt and pepper
300ml, ½pt milk
100g, 4oz Cheshire cheese, crumbled

Melt the butter in a saucepan and cook the onion until softened. Dice the potato and chop the broccoli. Add these to the saucepan and cook for several minutes. Pour in the stock, add the seasoning and bring to the boil. Cover and simmer for 30 minutes. Purée the mixture in a processor or blender and return to the saucepan. Add the milk and heat through. Pour the soup into bowls and top with the crumbled cheese.

PASTA WITH BROCCOLI, TUNA AND ANCHOVIES
Serves 4

350g, 12 oz pasta tubes
2 tbsp olive oil
2 cloves of garlic, peeled and chopped
4 anchovy fillets
½ tsp chilli flakes (optional)
225g, 8oz broccoli florets
1 red pepper
185g, 7oz can of tuna in sunflower or olive oil

Cook the pasta according to the packet instructions. To make the sauce add the garlic and anchovies to the oil in a frying pan. Fry for a couple of minutes and then stir in the broccoli, red pepper and chilli flakes if using. Cover and cook for a few minutes. Stir in the tuna with its oil. Pour over the drained pasta and serve immediately.

BROCCOLI AND DOLCELATTE FLAN
Serves 4 – 6

225g, 8oz shortcrust pastry
350g, 12oz broccoli florets
3 eggs
150ml, ¼pt milk
150ml, ¼pt single cream
75g, 3oz Dolcelatte cheese, crumbled

Roll out the pastry and use to line a greased 20cm, 8in flan dish. Bake blind in the oven at gas mark 4, 180°C (350°F) for 10 minutes. Blanch the broccoli florets for a couple of minutes in boiling water and then drain and refresh under cold water. Cut into fairly small pieces. Arrange over the base of the flan. Whisk together the eggs, milk and cream. Pour over the broccoli and arrange dolcelatte over the top. Return to the oven for 20 minutes.

BROCCOLI WITH EGG AND MUSHROOM
Serves 4 – 6

This is a tasty and nutritious dish and could be served with French bread or crusty rolls.

450g, 1lb broccoli, divided into florets and cut stalks
175g, 6oz mushrooms, sliced
1 clove of garlic, peeled and crushed
50g, 2oz butter
2 tbsp flour
150ml, ¼pt vegetable stock
150ml, ¼pt milk
4 hard-boiled eggs, halved
75g, 3oz mature Cheddar cheese, grated

Cook the broccoli until just tender and refresh under cold water to retain its green colour. Sauté the mushrooms in the butter and add the garlic. Mix in the flour and gradually stir in the stock and milk to make a smooth sauce. Stir in the broccoli florets. Transfer to a serving dish and arrange the halved eggs over the top. Scatter the cheese over the whole dish and put under the grill until golden and bubbling.

BROCCOLI AND TURKEY LASAGNE
Serves 4

225g, 8oz broccoli florets, sliced
25g, 1oz butter
25g, 1oz flour
300ml, ½pt milk
2 tbsp single cream
¼ tsp English mustard
450g, 1lb cooked turkey, diced
50g, 2oz cashew nuts, toasted
6 – 9 sheets of lasagne
100g, 4oz mozzarella cheese, sliced
100g, 4oz mature Cheddar cheese, grated

Blanch the broccoli in boiling water for a couple of minutes. Drain and refresh under cold water. To make the white sauce melt the butter, add the flour and gradually stir in the milk to make a smooth sauce. Stir in the cream and mustard and add the turkey and cashew nuts. Make layers in an ovenproof dish of the turkey mixture, then some broccoli and then 2 or 3 sheets of lasagne. Finish with a layer of sauce, top with the sliced mozzarella and sprinkle the Cheddar cheese over the top. Bake in the oven at gas mark 4, 180°C (350°F) for about 30 minutes until golden and bubbling.

BROCCOLI WITH ANCHOVY AND GARLIC
Serves 4 as a side dish

450g, 1lb broccoli florets
2 tbsp olive oil
5 anchovy fillets
1 garlic clove, peeled and crushed
1 tbsp toasted pine nuts

Steam the broccoli or cook in boiling, salted water for no longer than 2 or 3 minutes, since you need to retain some crunchiness. Drain and slice the florets into smaller pieces. Heat the olive oil in a small saucepan and add the anchovies and garlic. Stir over a low heat until the anchovies disintegrate. Mix in the broccoli and serve, scattered with pine nuts.

BROCCOLI IN CURRIED LEMON MAYONNAISE
Serves 4 as a side dish

450g, 1lb broccoli florets
1 tbsp soured cream
1 tsp curry powder

For the mayonnaise

2 egg yolks
1 tsp sugar
salt and black pepper
150ml, ¼pt olive oil
150ml, ¼pt sunflower oil
3 tbsp lemon juice

Cook the broccoli in a small amount of water or steam it until just tender and then drain it. To make the mayonnaise put the egg yolks, sugar and seasoning in a food processor and whiz for a few seconds. Start adding the oil, drip by drip and then in a slow steady trickle. Do not add it too fast or the mixture will curdle. When you have added about half of the oils you can add the lemon juice tablespoon by tablespoon. Then add the rest of the oil in the same way as before. You should have a thick, smooth mayonnaise. Mix the soured cream into the mayonnaise and add the curry powder to taste. Spoon the mayonnaise over the broccoli before serving.

PURPLE SPROUTING BROCCOLI
WITH TOMATO CREAM
Serves 4

450g, 1lb purple sprouting broccoli
3 tbsp cream cheese
1 tbsp tomato purée
150ml, ¼pt soured cream
8 cherry tomatoes, halved

Steam or cook the broccoli in a small amount of water until it is just tender – this will only take 3 or 4 minutes. Beat the cream cheese, stir in the tomato purée and soured cream. Fold in the halved tomatoes. Spoon over the broccoli and serve.

PURPLE SPROUTING BROCCOLI
WITH WALNUT BUTTER
Serves 3 – 4

450g, 1lb purple sprouting broccoli
50g, 2oz butter
25g, 1oz walnuts, crushed

Steam or cook the broccoli in a small amount of water until it is just tender – this will only take 3 or 4 minutes. In the meantime melt the butter in a small saucepan and cook until it turns brown. Tip in the walnuts and allow to heat through for 30 seconds. Transfer the broccoli to a serving dish and pour the walnut butter over the top. Serve at once.

BROCCOLI MUFFINS
Makes 10

These are nice served with bacon and eggs.

1 egg
240ml, 8fl oz milk
50g, 2oz melted butter
225g, 8oz self-raising flour
½ tsp mixed spice
350g, 12oz broccoli, chopped into small florets
100g, 4oz Cheddar cheese, grated

Whisk the egg, milk and butter together. Sift the flour and mixed spice together. Stir the egg mixture into the flour. Fold in the broccoli and the grated cheese. Spoon into greased muffin cases and bake in the oven at gas mark 5, 190°C (375°F) for 20 minutes or until well risen.

BRUSSELS SPROUTS

Brussels sprouts were first developed in Brussels in Belgium in the 1200s but it was not until the late 1800s that sprouts were grown in Britain. Britain is now the most important and climatically acceptable centre of production in the world. The plant is extremely hardy, enduring the coldest conditions and so ideal for the variable British winter.

Sprouts need a long season of growth and, unless you use manure and make sure the soil is very firm, you may not get a good crop. It can be disappointing to end up with only a few sprouts on each plant especially when they have occupied a lot of space in your vegetable patch. However you could be picking sprouts from October until March by using an early variety such as Peer Gynt F1 and a later variety such as Seven Hills, thereby spanning the coldest months of the year, and providing you with veg when other possibilities for greens are scarce. You can sow seeds in a cold frame in January and plant them out in May or June. Otherwise you can buy seedlings and plant them out in late spring. It is best to manure the ground the autumn before you plant your sprouts but do not disturb the soil after the end of January. Allow it to lie untouched until you plant your seedlings. You could possibly grow some radishes in the vacant space as these only have shallow roots. If the soil is not firm there is a danger that the sprouts will blow which means the leaves are not closely packed and the sprouts will not be firm. The sprout plant makes a tap root so the soil needs to have been dug deeply originally and the feeding roots form near the surface so benefit from well manured top soil. Once you have transplanted your seedlings to their final position it is possible to grow some quick maturing crops in between the sprout plants such as lettuces.

Individual sprouts develop on the stems from the bottom upwards. As you pick the sprouts strip the corresponding leaves from the stem. If the leaves turn yellow you must pick the sprouts and get rid of any yellow leaves at the same time. A good plant will produce sprouts very close together. Taller plants may need to be staked. One method of building up the sprouts is to pinch out the growing point which is about the size of a walnut in late autumn – this is known as 'cocking'.

One of the advantages of sprouts is that they yield their crop over a long period. You can remove a few sprouts from each plant as they become ready and leave those higher up the stem to mature. To pick the sprouts, snap the buttons off with a downward pressure of the thumb. The plants will develop a canopy of leaves at the top which resemble mini cabbages and can be picked and cooked as cabbages after you have picked all the sprouts. However if early sprouts are cut instead of picked you may be lucky and get a second crop that you can harvest after Christmas. I grew Icarus last year which seemed to be the only variety I could get as a plant. There are now various F1 Hybrids you can buy as seeds which produce a heavy crop over a longer period such as Peer Gynt F1 and Igor F1. There are also a couple of red varieties worth trying as they look very attractive, namely Falstaff or Rubine – they will remain red if you steam them but turn green if you boil them. Brussels sprouts are highly nutritious being an excellent source of fibre, folate and vitamin C. They also contain phytochemicals which fight against cancer.

BRUSSELS SPROUTS WITH
HAZELNUTS AND BACON
Serves 6

1kg, 2.2lb Brussels sprouts
225g, 8oz unsmoked back bacon, chopped
25g, 1oz butter
50g, 2oz hazelnuts

Steam the sprouts for 5 minutes. Melt the butter in a frying pan and fry the bacon and nuts until lightly browned. Add the sprouts and toss to combine. Cook gently for another 3 minutes. Serve at once.

BRUSSELS SPROUT SOUP
Serves 6

2 tbsp olive oil
1 onion, peeled and chopped
900ml, 1½pts vegetable stock
1 large potato, peeled and sliced
450g, 1lb Brussels sprouts, peeled
salt and pepper
4 tbsp double cream

Heat the olive oil in a frying pan and cook the onion for a few minutes until softened. Add the stock and potato and bring to the boil, then simmer for 10 minutes. Add the sprouts and boil for another 5 minutes. Do not overcook the sprouts. Leave to cool slightly and then purée in a blender or processor until smooth. Reheat, add salt and pepper and stir in the cream just before serving.

SPROUT OMELETTE
Serves 2

1 tbsp olive oil
knob of butter
100g, 4oz Brussels sprouts, peeled and sliced thinly
1 red pepper, halved, deseeded and sliced thinly
4 eggs, beaten
salt and pepper
1 tbsp fresh parsley, chopped

Heat the oil and butter in a large frying pan and add the sprouts and red pepper. Cook for only a couple of minutes before adding the eggs. Scatter over the parsley, salt and pepper. Cook the omelette until just set and either finish under the grill or fold over and finish cooking over a low heat. Serve at once.

SPROUTS WITH POPPY SEEDS AND LEMON
Serves 4

450g, 1lb Brussels sprouts, peeled and sliced
2 tbsp lemon juice
2 cloves of garlic, peeled and chopped
2 tbsp olive oil
dash of white wine
½ tbsp poppy seeds

Toss the sliced sprouts in the lemon juice. Heat the oil in a wok and stir fry the sprouts for a couple of minutes. Add the garlic and white wine and fry for 2 or 3 more minutes. Lastly, sprinkle with the poppy seeds and serve at once.

SPROUTS AND CARROTS
IN TOMATO CREAM SAUCE
Serves 2 – 3

225g, 8oz Brussels sprouts, peeled
1 large carrot, peeled and sliced
15g, ½oz butter
15g, ½oz plain flour
150ml, ¼pt vegetable stock
120ml, 4fl oz milk
1 tbsp tomato purée
25g, 1oz mature Cheddar cheese, grated

Steam the sprouts and carrots together for 5 minutes. Make the sauce by melting the butter, stirring in the flour and then gradually adding the stock, milk and tomato purée. Transfer the vegetables to a small ovenproof dish, cover with sauce and sprinkle the cheese on top. Finish off under a hot grill and serve at once.

SPROUTS WITH CHESTNUTS
Serves 4

450g, 1lb Brussels sprouts, peeled
25g, 1oz butter
225g, 8oz chestnuts, cooked

Steam the sprouts for about 5 minutes. Melt the butter in a saucepan and fry the chestnuts for a couple of minutes. Add the sprouts and toss with the chestnuts.

BRUSSELS SPROUT PURÉE
Serves 4

350g, 12oz Brussels sprouts, peeled
25g, 1oz brown breadcrumbs
2 tsp lemon juice
2 tbsp fromage frais
½ tsp ground nutmeg
salt and pepper

Cook the sprouts in boiling salted water for about 5 minutes. Drain but reserve the liquid. Put in a food processor with the breadcrumbs, lemon juice, fromage frais and seasonings. Process until smooth, adding a little of the reserved cooking liquid if the mixture is too dry. Reheat and serve.

CABBAGE

Cabbage, along with kale, cauliflower, broccoli, kohlrabi and Brussels sprouts all belong to the same species of plant: Brassica Oleracea, commonly known as Brassicas, which are all descended from the wild cabbage.

Cabbage has a long history, going back 4,000 years. Between China and Mongolia horsemen learned to preserve this vegetable in brine and it became the staple diet for the builders of the Great Wall of China. Greek mythology tells us that the cabbage actually sprang from the fallen tears of a Thracian king, Lycurgus, who was to be killed by Dionysus for uprooting some of his favourite grapevines. It was a popular vegetable in Greek and Roman times both as a food and for medicinal purposes. Cato (Roman Politician and General living around 200BC) said, *"The cabbage surpasses all other vegetables. If, at a banquet, you wish to dine a lot and enjoy your dinner, then eat as much cabbage as you wish, seasoned with vinegar, before dinner, and likewise after dinner eat some half-dozen leaves. It will make you feel as if you had not eaten, and you can drink as much as you like."*

The Celts may well have introduced cabbage to Britain in the 4th century BC. The cultivation of cabbage spread across northern Europe into Germany, Poland and Russia and became very popular. Sauerkraut, a dish made from fermented cabbage, was eaten by Dutch sailors during long voyages to prevent scurvy.

There are several types of cabbage. Spring cabbage has much looser leaves than other cabbage and is available from April to June. Summer cabbage is harvested in July and August and winter cabbage from October to March. The white leaved Dutch cabbage matures in the autumn. Savoy cabbages with their crinkly leaves are one of the best types of cabbage for cooking with – these are harvested from mid autumn to late winter. Chinese cabbage is also a brassica but you can eat it as a salad vegetable or use it like cooked cabbage – it can be harvested in August and September.

Cabbage can be a disappointing vegetable to grow because of the inevitable problems with caterpillars and slugs, not to mention pigeons. If you do decide you want to grow them you can plant seeds for summer cabbage outside from March to May – varieties recommended are Primo and Derby Day.

For winter cabbage which includes smooth skinned types and the hardy wrinkled Savoys sow outside in April or May for transplanting in July or early August spacing them 45cm, 18in apart – varieties are Christmas Drumhead, January King 3 and for the Savoys: Best of All.

For spring cabbage which can be either spring greens or hearted cabbage sow in early August in a seedbed and plant out in September at 10cm, 4in spacing, thinning to allow 30cm, 12in between plants. Spring Hero F1 is a recommended variety.

Cabbage is full of vitamin C and also an excellent source of Vitamins A, B and E. It is a good source of various minerals, in particular potassium. Raw cabbage is high in glutamine, an amino acid, important for intestinal health. People seem to have a general aversion to cabbage as a side vegetable but this is because it has the reputation of being overcooked, watery and giving off a nasty cabbagey smell. There is in fact nothing nicer than stir fried green cabbage or very lightly steamed shredded cabbage which retains all its nutrients and a good, crispy texture. If you are boiling cabbage, it is the sulphur compounds that are released which cause the nasty smell – a little vinegar added to the cooking water can help reduce the odour.

STUFFED CABBAGE LEAVES
Serves 3 – 4

12 cabbage leaves
450g, 1lb minced beef
25g, 1oz breadcrumbs
2 onions, peeled and sliced
1 garlic clove, peeled and crushed
½ tsp rosemary
½ tsp thyme
½ tsp marjoram
1 egg

Tomato sauce

300ml, ½pt Passata
pinch of chilli flakes
dash of Tabasco sauce

Blanch the cabbage leaves for 2 minutes in boiling water. Drain and lay them flat. Mix the mince with the breadcrumbs, onion, garlic and herbs and bind together with the egg. Lay each cabbage leaf flat and put a tablespoon of the mince mixture in the centre. Roll up one turn, fold the sides in and continue rolling until the leaf is a sausage shape. You may like to use a tooth pick to hold the cabbage parcels together. Grease a baking dish and lay the rolls in it closely packed together. Pour the tomato sauce over them and bake in the oven at gas mark 4, 180°C (350°F) for 40 minutes.

STIR FRIED CABBAGE WITH
SESAME SEEDS
Serves 3 – 4

Stir frying the cabbage helps retain all its nutrients and it tastes good too!

2 tbsp extra virgin olive oil
½ a green cabbage
1 tbsp sesame seeds
1 tbsp lemon juice

Shred the cabbage. Heat the oil in a wok and add the cabbage. Stir fry for a couple of minutes turning the cabbage over. Add the lemon juice, sprinkle with sesame seeds and serve at once.

STIR FRIED CABBAGE
WITH YOGHURT AND HORSERADISH
Serves 4

2 tbsp olive oil
1 spring cabbage
1 onion, peeled and sliced thinly
1 garlic clove, peeled and crushed
1 tbsp lemon juice
150ml, ¼pt Greek yoghurt
2 tsp creamed horseradish

Heat the oil in a wok. Shred the cabbage and stir fry in the wok with the onion and garlic. Keep turning the cabbage so that it doesn't burn. Mix together the lemon juice, yoghurt and horseradish. Drain the cabbage, getting rid of as much excess oil as possible. Mix in the yoghurt mixture and serve.

SWEET AND SOUR CABBAGE
Serves 3 – 4

½ a Savoy cabbage, shredded
2 tbsp sesame oil
1 tsp cornflour
1 tbsp sugar
4 tbsp water
2 tbsp soya sauce
1 tbsp tomato purée
1 tbsp white wine vinegar

Stir fry the cabbage in a wok, tossing it around in the oil on a high heat at first and then lower the heat, cover and cook for 5 minutes. Meanwhile mix the cornflour with a little of the water and then mix in all the other ingredients and heat for a couple of minutes. Stir into the cabbage and allow to heat through before serving.

CABBAGE STEAMED IN THE WOK
Serves 4 – 6

This is cabbage which is stir fried/steamed in the wok without oil making it a healthy and tasty way to serve cabbage.

1 spring cabbage, shredded
90ml, 3fl oz vegetable stock
1 tbsp sunflower seeds

Put the shredded cabbage in a wok and add the stock. Cover and allow to steam for 5 – 8 minutes. Add the sunflower seeds, give it a good stir and serve.

CREAMY CABBAGE BAKE
Serves 4

½ a green cabbage, shredded
2 eggs, beaten
150ml, ¼pt Greek yoghurt
100g, 4oz Edam cheese, grated
25g, 1oz brown breadcrumbs
2 tbsp Parmesan or mature Cheddar cheese, grated

Steam the cabbage for a few minutes – not for too long so that it still has some crunch. Mix together the eggs and yoghurt and stir in the grated cheese. Combine this mixture with the cabbage and transfer to an ovenproof dish. Sprinkle the breadcrumbs and Parmesan on top and bake in the oven at gas mark 5, 190°C (375°F) for 15 minutes or until the top is nicely browned.

BUBBLE AND SQUEAK
Serves 4

225g, 8oz potatoes, cooked and mashed
225g, 8oz green cabbage, shredded and steamed
salt and pepper
2 tbsp olive oil
1 tsp vinegar

Mix the potato and cabbage together and season with salt and pepper. Heat the olive oil in a large frying pan and add the potato and cabbage mixture. Cook for several minutes, tossing and turning the mixture until heated through. Sprinkle the vinegar on top and serve at once.

CARROTS

The carrot originated in Afghanistan about 5,000 years ago - at this time carrots were purple, white, red, yellow, green or black but not orange. In Roman times we know they had purple or white carrots. Arab merchants travelling the trade routes of Africa, Arabia and Asia brought the purple seeds home with them and then it is thought Moorish invaders brought the purple and yellow varieties of carrots from North Africa to Southern Europe around the twelfth century and by the thirteenth century carrots were being grown in France and Germany. Flemish refugees eventually introduced the yellow and purple carrot to England in the fifteenth century. The Elizabethans used carrot tops instead of feathers to decorate their hats and brooches.

Orange carrots were developed in Holland in the 1700s by patriotic Dutchmen who wanted to grow them in the colours of the House of Orange. Pale yellow versions were crossed with red varieties which contained anthocyanin and thus produced orange-coloured roots.

Carrots need a light, sandy, free-draining soil. If you are hoping to grow long carrots the lighter the soil and the less stones the better. For the short stumpy varieties most soils will do but it is best not to use fresh manure as this can cause the carrots to fork. Carrots in general do not germinate well if the soil is too cold so it is best to wait until mid spring before sowing seeds. Germination time is usually about 17 days. Carrots sown in May will be ready in September or early October.

You will need to thin out the seedlings so that each carrot is about 5 – 7cm, 2 – 3 in apart. Carrots should not be over watered as this can lead to rapid leaf growth at the expense of root growth. Nor should carrots be allowed to become too dry especially as, if you then water them extensively, you will cause the roots to split. If you want to grow really large, prize winning carrots you should use the crow bar method. You make a 60cm, 2ft hole in the ground with a crow bar. Make a circular movement in the hole to create a funnel shape. Then fill the hole with John Innes compost and plant a few seeds in a circle at the top. Cover with a little compost. Thin to the strongest seedling once the seeds have germinated.

Varieties to be recommended are Amsterdam Forcing and Early Nantes which are short rooted early carrots (these can be sown around the end of March). For the maincrop try Chantenay, James Scarlet Intermediate or Autumn King and for late crops try St Valery which is long rooted or Flakkee which is Dutch and a large thick carrot.

Carrot fly is the most troublesome of pests that can affect carrots. The flies lay their eggs in the soil and the larvae burrow into the carrots. There is no treatment for this problem but there are resistant cultivars on the market. Intercropping carrots with onions can reduce carrot fly. As your carrots develop the sunlight may cause them to go green at the top - if so cover them with a little earth.

Carrots contain the richest source of beta-carotene which is converted by the liver in the body to vitamin A, a lack of which is alleged to cause poor night vision. Carrots contain antioxidants, helping fight against cancer and heart disease. They are rich in various minerals including sodium, sulphur, chlorine and contain traces of iodine. These minerals lie very close to the skin so if possible you should scrub the carrots to get rid of any dirt rather than peeling them. Carrots contain about 7% natural sugar and are therefore useful in sweet recipes such as carrot cakes.

Carrots are the one vegetable that do you more good if eaten cooked rather than raw as the beta-carotene is more easily absorbed when heated. Cooked carrots contain up to three times more antioxidants than raw carrots.

CARROT, TOMATO AND LEMON SOUP
Serves 6

3 tbsp sunflower oil + knob of butter
2 onions, peeled and chopped
450g, 1lb carrots, scrubbed and chopped
400g, 14oz tin of tomatoes
grated rind and juice of 2 lemons
1.2 litres, 2pts chicken stock
salt and pepper
6 tbsp natural yoghurt + parsley for garnish

Heat the oil and butter together in a saucepan and fry the onions for about 5 minutes. Add the carrots and then the tomatoes, lemon rind and stock. Bring up to a simmer and half-covering the pan, simmer for about 30 minutes. Leave to cool a little and then process. Pour through a sieve into a clean saucepan, stir in the lemon juice and reheat before serving. Swirl a spoonful of yoghurt into each bowl of soup and garnish with parsley.

CARROT AND LENTIL SOUP
Serves 4

2 tbsp olive oil
1 onion, scrubbed and chopped
2 carrots, scrubbed or peeled and sliced
1 clove of garlic, peeled and chopped
100g, 4oz red lentils
600ml, 1pt vegetable stock
100g, 4oz Boursin cheese
1 tbsp fresh parsley, chopped

Fry the onion and carrot in the oil in a saucepan for a few minutes and add the garlic. Stir in the red lentils and then add the vegetable stock. Bring to the boil, cover and simmer, stirring occasionally for 30 minutes. Serve hot in bowls adding a little dollop of Boursin and a sprinkling of parsley to each portion.

CARROT AND APPLE COLESLAW
Serves 6 - 8

2 eating apples, cored and sliced
2 carrots, scrubbed and grated
225g, 8oz white cabbage, finely shredded
½ an onion, peeled and grated
2 tbsp mayonnaise
2 tbsp olive oil
1 tbsp white wine vinegar
salt and pepper
1 clove of garlic, peeled and crushed

Combine the first 4 ingredients. Add the mayonnaise and a dressing made by mixing the oil and vinegar together with the salt, pepper and a clove of crushed garlic.

CARROT, CHEESE AND TARRAGON SOUFFLÉ
Serves 4

450g, 1lb carrots, scrubbed and chopped
25g, 1oz butter
25g, 1oz plain flour
4 eggs, separated
50g, 2oz mature Cheddar cheese, grated
1 tsp chopped tarragon

Cook the carrots in boiling water, purée them and reserve the liquid. Melt the butter in a saucepan and stir in the flour. Gradually add 150ml, ¼pt of the reserved water, stirring all the time until the sauce is smooth. Stir in the carrot purée and egg yolks one at a time, the tarragon and the cheese. Whisk the egg whites until stiff and with a metal spoon gently fold them into the mixture. Pour into a greased soufflé dish and cook in a preheated oven at gas mark 5, 190°C (375°F) for 30 minutes. Serve immediately.

CHICKEN, CARROT AND LEMON PIE
Serves 4

50g, 2oz butter
1 onion, peeled and sliced
675g, 1½lb carrots, peeled and diced
100g, 4oz mushrooms, chopped
100g, 4oz courgettes, diced
40g, 1½oz flour
150ml, ¼pt chicken stock
grated rind and juice of 1 lemon
salt and pepper
350g, 12oz cooked chicken meat, diced
150ml, ¼pt single cream
175g, 6oz shortcrust pastry

Melt the butter in a casserole and fry the onion and carrots for 10 minutes. Add the mushrooms and courgettes and fry for a further 5 minutes. Remove the vegetables. Blend the flour into the butter remaining in the casserole and gradually stir in the stock, lemon rind and juice. Bring to the boil, season and add the chicken and vegetables. Gradually stir in the cream and then transfer to a pie dish. Roll out the pastry and use to cover the pie, making a few holes with a skewer to allow steam to escape. Bake in the oven at gas mark 5, 190°C (375°F) for at least 30 minutes until the pastry is golden brown.

CARROT AND PARSNIP FRITTERS
Serves 4

100g, 4oz self-raising flour
1 egg
150ml, ¼pt milk
1 tsp olive oil
225g, 8oz carrots, scrubbed, diced and cooked
225g, 8oz parsnips, peeled, diced and cooked
1 tbsp fresh parsley, chopped
sunflower oil for frying

Make up the batter by mixing the milk and egg into the flour and stirring in the oil. Stir in the cooked parsnips, carrots and parsley. Heat oil in a large frying pan and drop spoonfuls of the mixture into the pan. Fry fritters until browned on both sides. This mixture should make about 16 small fritters.

GLAZED CARROTS WITH HAZELNUTS
Serves 4

450g, 1lb carrots, scrubbed, halved and sliced lengthways
3 tbsp caster sugar
2 tbsp water
25g, 1oz butter
1 tbsp hazelnuts, chopped

Steam the carrots for no longer than 5 minutes. Heat the water and sugar in a saucepan. Add the butter and stir to melt. Add the carrots and cook over a low heat for 10 minutes, turning the carrots every so often. Sprinkle with the hazelnuts and serve immediately.

CARROT AND KALE WITH POPPY SEEDS
Serves 4 - see photo in colour section

450g, 1lb carrots, scrubbed and sliced into sticks
bunch of curly kale, leaves separated
15g, ½oz butter
1 tbsp poppy seeds

Cook the carrots in salted water for between 5 and 8 minutes. Steam the kale for 3 or 4 minutes. Mix together in a serving dish with the butter. Sprinkle with poppy seeds and serve.

CARROT AND APPLE TART
Serves 4 - see photo in colour section

This makes an interesting and healthy tart. Serve with single cream.

175g, 6oz shortcrust pastry
25g, 1oz brown breadcrumbs
50g, 2oz carrot, grated
2 eating apples, cored, peeled and grated
50g, 2oz butter, melted
150ml, ¼pt single cream
1 tbsp lemon juice
50g, 2oz caster sugar
1 whole egg and 1 egg yolk

Line a 17.5cm, 7in greased flan tin with the pastry. Put the breadcrumbs, carrot and apple in a mixing bowl and beat in the butter, cream, lemon juice, sugar, whole egg and egg yolk. When all is thoroughly combined pour onto the pastry base and bake in the oven on a baking tray (this helps prevent the pastry becoming soggy) at gas mark 4, 180°C (350°F) for 25 minutes.

CARROT MUFFINS
Makes 12 muffins

275g, 10oz self-raising flour
1 tsp bicarbonate of soda
1 egg
90ml, 3fl oz milk
2 tbsp clear honey
5oz, 125g light muscovado sugar
350g, 12 oz carrots, scrubbed and grated
1 tsp vanilla essence
75g, 3oz butter, melted

Sift together the flour and bicarbonate of soda. Whisk the egg and add the milk, honey, sugar, carrot and vanilla essence and lastly the melted butter. Stir well and pour onto the flour. Beat until the mixture is smooth and spoon into greased muffin tins. Bake in the oven at gas mark 5, 190°C (375°F) for 20 minutes or until well risen.

CARROT CAKE
WITH LEMON AND LIME FILLING
Serves 6

175g, 6oz wholemeal flour
2 tsp baking powder
100g, 4oz carrot, peeled and grated
100g, 4oz butter
100g, 4oz light brown sugar
2 eggs
2 tbsp milk

Filling

100g, 4oz cream cheese
25g, 1oz butter
grated rind of ½ lemon and 1 lime
½ tsp vanilla essence
200g, 7oz icing sugar

You can put all the ingredients in a food processor and whiz until smooth. Alternatively sift together the flour and baking powder. Add the grated carrot. Cream the butter and brown sugar together. Beat the eggs and add to the mixture, adding a little flour if the mixture begins to curdle. Gradually add all the flour and carrot and mix in the milk. Divide the cake mixture between 2 greased 15cm, 6in cake tins. Bake in the oven at gas mark 4, 180°C (350°F) for 25 minutes. Meanwhile make the filling by beating together the butter and cream cheese. Add the grated rind and beat in the icing sugar and vanilla essence. Use this filling to sandwich the cakes together. Dust with icing sugar and serve.

STICKY TOFFEE PUDDING
WITH CARROTS
Serves 6

75g, 3oz dates, chopped
120ml, 4fl oz water
½ tsp bicarbonate of soda
75g, 3oz butter
125g, 5oz light brown sugar
2 eggs
175g, 6oz self-raising flour
75g, 3oz carrot, grated

Butterscotch sauce

50g, 2oz butter
50g, 2oz dark brown sugar
200ml, 7fl oz single cream

Put the dates and water in a small saucepan and bring to the boil. Sprinkle the bicarbonate of soda on the top and set aside. Cream together the butter and sugar. Beat in the eggs. Stir in the flour and lastly fold in the grated carrot and dates with the liquid. Divide the mixture between 6 small greased pudding basins and place on a baking tray in a preheated oven at gas mark 4, 180°C (350°F) for 25 minutes. Meanwhile make the butterscotch sauce by melting the butter and sugar together. Stir in the cream and allow to bubble for 2 or 3 minutes. Turn out the puddings and pour the sauce over them or serve it separately.

CARROT MARMALADE
Makes about 2kg, 4½lb

225g, 8oz carrots, peeled
1 medium orange
2 medium lemons
1½ litres, 3pts water
1.5kg, 3lb granulated sugar
½ tsp cinnamon

Finely chop the carrots and put them in a preserving pan. Wash the orange and lemons and cut each one in half. Squeeze out the juice, remove the pith from the peel and shred the peel finely. Chop the pith roughly and place with the pips in a muslin bag. Place the shredded peel, juice and muslin bag in the pan with the carrots. Add the water, bring to the boil, cover and simmer gently for 1½ hours, until the peel is soft. Squeeze any juice you can out of the muslin bag and remove it. The pith and pips contain the pectin that you need for your marmalade to set. Add the sugar and stir until dissolved, then stir in the cinnamon. Now boil rapidly until setting point is reached. This should take no more than 15 minutes. To test for a set, drop a small spoonful onto a cold saucer. If, when you push the liquid with your finger, the surface wrinkles, you have a set. Remove any scum and allow to cool, stirring gently to prevent a skin forming. Pour into warmed, sterilized jars and seal.

CAULIFLOWER

Cauliflower is thought to have originated in the Middle East and more particularly in Cyprus. It was known as the Cole-Flower. It was definitely being grown in Britain by the late 1700s as Dr Johnson referred to it, 'Of all the flowers in the garden I like the cauliflower.' But Mark Twain wrote rather scathingly, 'Cauliflower is nothing but cabbage with a college education'.

There are two types of cauliflower; the cauliflower proper which is harvested in summer and early autumn, and winter cauliflower which is actually broccoli and grown for an October to June harvest (see broccoli on page 24).

Cauliflowers are not that easy to grow but worth a try. They do take up quite a lot of space providing you with only one cauliflower per plant. It is easiest to buy seedlings in the spring and grow them on. If you want to grow your cauliflowers from seed, summer varieties need to be sown in October in a cold frame and planted out in March. Autumn varieties need to be sown outdoors after mid-May for planting out in July leaving about 60cm, 2ft between seedlings. They need a rich and deep soil and must be kept watered right through from germination until harvest - any check in growth will prevent good, rounded curds forming.

The cauliflowers should be picked as soon as the florets look white and firm. Several varieties have leaves that curl over the florets to prevent them getting scorched in the sun. If you are growing a variety with upright leaves it is a good idea to break a leaf or two and bend it over the florets yourself. If left too long in the ground the heads will go yellow and not be worth bothering about. Harvest by cutting through the stem so that several leaves are left surrounding the florets but the older leaves are left on the stalk. If you have too many cauliflowers maturing at the same time you can lift them with their roots, tie the stems together with twine and hang them head downwards in a cool shed. Spray them with water every so often and they should maintain their freshness.

Surprisingly India is the largest producer of cauliflowers. Cauliflower is a good source of Vitamin C, potassium and fibre. It also contains several phytochemicals including the cancer-fighting glucosinolates. It is a versatile vegetable that can be served cold with mayonnaise or vinaigrette as part of a salad, turned into soup, stir fried, used as crudités for dips, pickled or of course turned into a cauliflower cheese. When cooking cauliflower adding a little sugar to the salted, boiling water will help bring out its flavour and keep it white.

CHEESY CAULIFLOWER SOUP
Serves 4 – 6

1 cauliflower, divided into florets
600ml, 1pt milk
750ml, 1¼pts vegetable stock
25g, 1oz butter
2 tbsp flour
salt and pepper
50g, 2oz mature Cheddar cheese, grated
1 tbsp fresh parsley, chopped

Steam a few small florets for 5 minutes and then set aside. Chop up the rest and put in a saucepan with the milk and 450ml, ¾pt of the stock. Bring to the boil and then simmer covered for 10 minutes. Purée the mixture in a blender. In a small saucepan melt the butter, stir in the flour and then gradually add the rest of the stock. Stir until smooth and then add the puréed mixture. Season with salt and pepper and stir in the cheese. Just before serving add the little florets and scatter with parsley.

CAULIFLOWER SALAD
Serves 4 - 6

This is a filling and very tasty salad. It would go down well as part of a cold buffet lunch.

3 red-skinned eating apples, cored and thinly sliced
2 tbsp lemon juice
1 crisp lettuce, shredded
1 cauliflower, broken into florets
100g, 4oz garlic sausage, cut into strips
300ml, ½pt mayonnaise
150ml, ¼pt soured cream
1 tbsp curry powder

Sprinkle the apple slices with lemon juice and place in a large salad bowl with the lettuce, cauliflower and sausage. Blend the mayonnaise, soured cream and curry powder together and pour over the salad just before serving.

CAULIFLOWER FLORETS WITH OLIVE OIL AND LEMON DRESSING
Serves 3 – 4

½ a cauliflower
3 tbsp olive oil
1 tbsp lemon juice
salt and pepper
1 tbsp fresh parsley, chopped

Break up the cauliflower into florets and steam for about 5 minutes so that they still have some bite. Transfer to a serving dish and while still warm stir in the olive oil and lemon juice. Season and scatter the parsley over the cauliflower.

HOT CAULIFLOWER AND CARROT SALAD
Serves 4

225g, 8oz cauliflower florets
100g, 4oz carrots, peeled and sliced into sticks
1 tbsp olive oil
3 tbsp mayonnaise
1 tsp lemon juice
1 tsp poppy seeds

Lightly cook the cauliflower and carrots so that they are still crunchy. Transfer to a serving dish and mix in the olive oil, mayonnaise and lemon juice. Sprinkle with poppy seeds and serve while still warm.

CAULIFLOWER AND STILTON SOUFFLÉ
Serves 3 – 4

25g, 1oz butter
25g, 1oz plain flour
180ml, 6fl oz milk
100g, 4oz Stilton cheese, crumbled
1 tsp dried sage or 2 tsp fresh sage
225g, 8oz cauliflower, divided into small florets
3 eggs, separated

Melt the butter in a saucepan and add the flour. Gradually add the milk, stirring all the time until smooth and bring to a simmer. Add the cheese and sage. When the cheese has melted remove from the heat. Meanwhile steam the cauliflower for no more than 5 minutes. Fold the egg yolks into the cheese sauce and then fold in the cauliflower. Allow to cool. Whisk the egg whites until stiff and then carefully fold them into the cauliflower mixture. Spoon into a greased 1litre, 1.75pt soufflé dish. Bake in the oven at gas mark 6, 200°C (400°F) for 35 minutes by which time the soufflé should be well risen and golden brown.

CAULIFLOWER POLONAISE
Serves 4 – 6

1 cauliflower, divided into florets
50g, 2oz butter
50g, 2oz brown breadcrumbs
1 clove of garlic, peeled and crushed
2 eggs, hard-boiled and chopped
1 tbsp fresh parsley, chopped
sprinkling of black pepper

Cook the cauliflower in boiling water until just tender. Arrange in a serving bowl. Melt the butter in a small saucepan and fry the breadcrumbs and garlic for a few minutes. Add the chopped egg, parsley and pepper and sprinkle over the cauliflower. Serve immediately.

CURRIED CAULIFLOWER
Serves 4 – 6 as a side dish

2 tbsp olive oil
½ tsp mustard seeds
1 tbsp ginger root, peeled and finely chopped
pinch of cumin seeds
2 onions, peeled and chopped
½ tsp turmeric
1 cauliflower, divided into florets
2 tomatoes, chopped
2 green chillis, deseeded and chopped

Heat the oil in a frying pan and add the mustard seeds, ginger, cumin seeds and onion. Fry for a couple of minutes, then add the turmeric and cook for a couple more minutes. Add the cauliflower and stir to coat in the spicy mixture. Add the tomatoes and chilli and a little water and cook until the cauliflower is tender.

CAULIFLOWER CHEESE
WITH BACON AND ONIONS
Serves 3 – 4

This is almost a meal in itself.

½ a cauliflower
15g, ½oz butter
1 small onion, peeled and chopped
100g, 4oz unsmoked back bacon, diced
15g, ½oz margarine
1 tbsp flour
150ml, ¼pt milk
½ tsp dry mustard
100g, 4oz mature Cheddar cheese, grated

Break the cauliflower into florets and cook in boiling water for 5 minutes. Drain and place in a small ovenproof dish. Melt the butter in a small frying pan and fry the onion and bacon until crisp. Scatter over the cauliflower. Make a white sauce by melting the margarine in a small saucepan and stirring in the flour. Gradually add the milk, stirring all the time until you have a smooth sauce. Mix in the mustard. Pour over the cauliflower and scatter the grated cheese over the top. Cook in a preheated oven at gas mark 4, 180°C (350°F) for 20 minutes or until browned on top.

CAULIFLOWER WITH MUSHROOMS
Serves 4 – 6

2 tbsp olive oil
1 cauliflower, divided into florets
50g, 2oz mushrooms
150ml, ¼pt vegetable stock
2 egg yolks
¼ tsp cornflour
2 tbsp single cream
15g, ½oz butter
2 tbsp brown breadcrumbs

Fry the mushrooms and cauliflower in the oil in a saucepan for several minutes. Add the stock, cover and simmer for a further 5 minutes. Strain the stock into another saucepan. Beat the cornflour into the egg yolks, mix with the cream and add to the stock. Cook, stirring until the mixture thickens. Pour over the cauliflower and mushrooms arranged in serving dish. Fry the breadcrumbs in the butter and sprinkle over the top.

CAULIFLOWER FRITTERS
Serves 4 – 6

These go well with a tomato sauce for a vegetarian meal or otherwise with a fish or meat dish.

1 cauliflower, divided into florets
oil for deep frying

Batter
4 tbsp flour
1 egg, beaten
180ml, 6fl oz beer

To make the batter mix all the ingredients together in a food processor or put the flour in a bowl, make a well in the centre and gradually incorporate the egg and beer. Stir until you have a smooth batter. Dip the florets in the batter and fry them in hot oil until golden and crisp.

CAULIFLOWER PICKLE

1 large cauliflower
1 tbsp salt
1 shallot, peeled and chopped
1 dried chilli, chopped
8 peppercorns
½ tsp allspice
2.5cm, 1in root ginger
1.2 litres, 2 pts vinegar

Sprinkle the cauliflower florets with the salt and leave for 24 hours. This will get rid of the moisture. Now put them into a couple of large jars. To make the pickling vinegar put the chopped shallot, chilli, and other ingredients in the vinegar and bring to the boil. Simmer for 15 minutes, then strain and pour over the cauliflower in the jars. Leave for a few weeks before using.

CELERY AND CELERIAC

Celery was cultivated and eaten by the Greeks and Romans; the ancient Egyptians only used it for ritual purposes. Celery was developed and improved in Italy during the 1600s but it was not until the 1800s that it was introduced to other parts of Europe including Britain. Italian gardeners had learnt to cultivate blanched celery by covering it with mounds of earth to keep out the light. Celery is a biennial plant and a relation of celeriac. Celeriac originated in the Mediterranean region, being introduced to Britain in the 1700s. It tastes like celery but differs in that it concentrates its energies into producing a swollen bulb-like root. The leafy stalks can also be eaten and are similar to sea kale.

There are two types of celery that you can grow. You can either raise plants from seed or you can buy plants in the spring from your Garden Centre. Trench celery gives an excellent crop but is the most difficult to grow, needing plenty of space and maintenance. It is planted in a trench to which well rotted manure has been added. Plants should be planted out when they are about 15cm, 6in tall. Earthing up takes place in three stages, with about two weeks between each. As the celery grows you mound the earth round the stems so that they are deprived of light.

Self-blanching celery is easier to grow. It doesn't need earthing up but must be grown in a block of plants so that the lack of light causes most of the plants to go white. Regular watering is essential and beware of slugs who love celery.

Celeriac is the easiest of all to grow. You can raise plants from seed in March. Plant out in May allowing 30cm, 12in between seedlings and 45cm, 18in between rows. As the roots swell draw the soil away from them so that they have room to expand. Cut off any suckers that develop. When there is a danger of frost draw the soil around the roots again. They can be left in the ground all winter and harvested as you need them or they also store well in boxes of sand or soil.

Celery is rich in Vitamin A. It is an ideal vegetable for slimmers, being very low in calories.

WALDORF SALAD
Serves 4

This classic recipe was created by Oscar, the maître d'hôtel at the Waldorf Astoria Hotel in New York in the early 1900s.

450g, 1lb red-skinned eating apples, cored
juice of ½ a lemon
4 celery stalks
150ml, ¼pt mayonnaise
75g, 3oz walnuts, chopped

Slice the apples and sprinkle with lemon juice to prevent them going brown. Chop the celery finely and add to the apples in a serving dish. Mix in the mayonnaise and the walnuts and serve.

BRAISED CELERY WITH PINE NUTS
Serves 4

1 large head of celery, trimmed and washed
50g, 2oz butter
1 onion, peeled and chopped
1 carrot, peeled and cut into circles
150ml, ¼pt vegetable stock
50g, 2oz pine nuts
1 tbsp fresh parsley, chopped

Cut the celery into sticks about 2.5cm, 1in thick. Melt the butter in a saucepan and add the celery, onion and carrot. Cook for about 5 minutes and then add the stock, cover and simmer for 20 minutes. Stir in the nuts and heat through. Turn into a serving dish and sprinkle with the parsley.

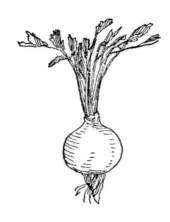

CELERIAC AND POTATO PURÉE
Serves 4

225g, 8oz celeriac, peeled, cooked and chopped
225g, 8oz potatoes, peeled, cooked and chopped
salt and pepper
50g, 2oz butter

Mash the celeriac and potato together, add the seasoning and mix in the butter.

CELERIAC SALAD
Serves 3 – 4

1 small celeriac, peeled
½ bulb of fennel
1 onion, peeled and chopped
1 eating apple, peeled and chopped
1 bunch of watercress

Dressing

6 tbsp olive oil
2 tbsp white wine vinegar
1 tbsp lemon juice
1 tsp honey
salt and pepper

Cut the celeriac and the fennel into thin strips. Place in a serving bowl and add the onion and apple. To make the dressing combine all the ingredients, stir together and pour over the salad. Add the watercress just before serving.

CELERIAC REMOULADE
Serves 4 – 6

450g, 1lb celeriac, peeled and cut into strips
2 tbsp Dijon mustard
3 tbsp mayonnaise
1 tsp lemon juice
3 tbsp soured cream
1 tsp chopped parsley
1 tsp chopped chives

Blanch the celeriac in boiling water for 2 minutes. Drain and transfer to a serving bowl. Blend the mustard with the mayonnaise, lemon juice and soured cream. Fold into the celeriac and sprinkle with the parsley and chives.

CHICORY, RADICCHIO AND ENDIVE

It is thought that endive was eaten by the Egyptians but it was definitely well known to the Romans and is mentioned by Ovid, Horace and Pliny. It wasn't introduced to Europe until the 1500s. Chicory also has a long history and was referred to by Pliny.

There are three types of chicory – red chicory or radicchio which has been introduced comparatively recently from Italy. The lower temperatures in the autumn/winter make their leaves turn a beautiful crimson although there are now some varieties which are naturally red and heart earlier. The second type is the 'forcing' chicory such as Witloof which produces leafy heads, known as chicons when blanched. This form of chicory has a large taproot and it is this root which can be roasted, ground or used as a coffee substitute. Then there are non-forcing or sugarloaf types which produce large hearted lettuce-like heads for autumn and winter harvesting. Try Pan di Zucchero.

There are two types of endive – batavian or escarole is an upright plant with large, broad leaves. Then there is curly endive with serrated leaves which can be harvested in the summer and added to salads. The leaves are slightly bitter.

Endive and radicchio can be grown in the same way as lettuces and recommended varieties of radicchio are Palla Rossa and Rossa di Verona. For curly or frizzy endives try Pancalieri or Wallonne and for a batavian type try Grobo. Chicory grown for the chicons has to be forced which means you need to sow seeds in June and lift the roots in October - you then cut the leaves off and trim up the bottom of the roots. You plant the roots in deep pots in moist sandy soil and leave them in the dark - chicons should have formed after 4 weeks.

Chicory contains the nutrient inulin which is known to promote good bacteria and helps detox the colon. Radicchio, like broccoli, contains glucosinolates, the phytochemicals which break down into a substance called sulforaphane (said to have a strong anti-cancer effect).

ENDIVE, EGG AND ANCHOVY SALAD
Serves 3 – 4

1 head of endive
50g, 2oz tin of anchovy fillets
4 hard-boiled eggs
1 tbsp white wine vinegar
3 tbsp olive oil

Drain the anchovies of oil and mash up with 2 of the eggs. Add the vinegar and oil and stir together. Leave to stand for 30 minutes. Tear up the endive leaves and arrange them in a serving bowl. Pour the anchovy sauce over them. Slice the remaining eggs and arrange on top.

BRAISED ENDIVE
Serves 2 – 3

1 head of endive, cut into quarters
1 tbsp lemon juice
2 tbsp vegetable stock
1 tsp sugar
25g, 1oz butter
1 tsp flour

Put the endive into a small casserole with the lemon juice, stock, sugar and half the butter. Cover and cook for 20 minutes. Remove the endive and keep warm in a serving dish. Mix the rest of the butter with the flour and stir into the liquid left in the pan. Pour over the endive and serve.

CHICORY IN MUSTARD SAUCE
Serves 4

This goes well with grilled meat or fish.

4 heads chicory
150ml, ¼pt water
juice of 1 lemon
15g, ½oz butter
1 tbsp flour
150ml, ¼pt vegetable stock
3 tbsp single cream
2 tbsp Dijon mustard
1 tsp sugar
1 tbsp dill, chopped

Wash the heads of chicory and remove the thick stems. Bring the water to the boil and add the lemon juice. Tip in the chicory and simmer for 5 minutes. Drain but reserve the cooking liquid. Melt the butter in a small saucepan and stir in the flour. Gradually add the reserved liquid and the stock, stirring all the time. Add the cream, mustard and sugar. Transfer the chicory to an ovenproof dish and pour over the sauce. Cook for a further 10 minutes in the oven at gas mark 3, 160°C (325°F).

CHICORY AU GRATIN
Serves 4

This goes well with gammon or ham.

4 heads of chicory
juice of 1 lemon
4 tbsp olive oil
2 tsp mint, chopped
salt and pepper
3 tbsp double cream
175g, 6oz mozzarella cheese, sliced

Cut the chicory into thick rings and sprinkle with lemon juice. Stir the mint, salt and pepper into the oil and fold in the cream. Pour over the chicory and spoon into an ovenproof dish. Arrange the sliced mozzarella cheese over the top and cook in the oven at gas mark 6, 200°C (400°F) for about 15 minutes.

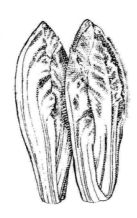

CHICORY, AVOCADO AND TOMATO SALAD
Serves 2 – 3

1 head of chicory
1 avocado, peeled and sliced
2 tomatoes, quartered
1 red pepper, deseeded and sliced

Walnut dressing

5 tbsp olive oil
1 tbsp lemon juice
1 tbsp red wine vinegar
1 tsp mild French mustard
1 tsp sugar
salt and pepper
25g, 1oz walnuts, crushed

Cut the chicory in half and discard the central stem and the base. Separate the leaves and arrange in a serving bowl. Arrange the avocado, tomatoes and red pepper over the chicory. To make the dressing combine all the ingredients in a screw-topped jar and shake. Mix the nuts into the dressing when you are ready to serve and pour over the salad ingredients.

PRAWN, APPLE AND RADICCHIO SALAD
Serves 3 – 4

100g, 4oz radicchio leaves
225g, 8oz prawns, shelled
225g, 8oz green eating apples, cored and sliced
4 tbsp apple juice
1 tsp fresh mint, chopped

2 tsp vinegar
1 tsp caster sugar

Arrange the radicchio leaves on a serving plate. Mix together the prawns and apples. Lay over the radicchio. Pour the apple juice over them. Mix together the vinegar, mint and sugar and sprinkle over the apples and prawns.

RADICCHIO, EGG AND AVOCADO SALAD
Serves 3 – 4   - see photo in colour section

A popular salad with the family.

½ a radicchio
3 hard-boiled eggs, halved
1 avocado, peeled and sliced
1 tomato, chopped
100g, 4oz sweetcorn
1 tbsp sunflower seeds

Creamy dressing

1 tbsp caster sugar
2 tbsp lemon juice
1 tsp Dijon mustard
pinch of paprika
120ml, 4fl oz crème fraîche

Separate the radicchio leaves and arrange in a serving dish. Slice the eggs and arrange over the leaves along with the avocado and tomato. Scatter sweetcorn and sunflower seeds over the salad. Make the dressing by mixing together the sugar, lemon juice, mustard and paprika with some salt and pepper. Stir in the crème fraîche and chill. Just before serving, pour the dressing over the salad.

COURGETTES AND MARROWS

Courgettes and marrows are closely related to squashes and pumpkins. The courgette is a variety of vegetable marrow (really just a small marrow) and is a very recently introduced vegetable in comparison to others. They arrived in this country after the Second World War from Italy where they are known as zucchini. They had probably been brought to Italy from Mexico.

Courgettes are relatively easy to grow and do well in grow bags. You can either buy seedlings in May from your local Garden Centre or grow them from seeds for transplanting once the last frosts have passed. Courgettes need a bed of rich compost and animal manure. They will need regular watering but it is best to water around the plants as watering over the plants may cause the fruits to rot. You will also have to protect against slugs. Plants carry separate male and female flowers. The male stalks are plain while the female bears the fruit. The female flowers must be pollinated for fruit to form - bumble bees usually do this for us - otherwise you can hand pollinate the female flowers by taking the male flower, stripping off the petals and bringing the anthers into contact with the female stigmas. Pick them while still small in August and September and the plants will keep producing more until the cold weather sets in and stops production. You can grow yellow skinned courgettes but their flavour is much the same as the green and you can also grow yellow or green round courgettes which are ideal for stuffing. If you want marrows, just leave the courgettes and they will grow large very quickly. Although courgettes are basically small marrows there are specific courgette varieties that have been bred to bear lots of small fruits instead of a few large marrows. Zucchini F1 is a recognised variety of courgette while Long Green Trailing is a marrow variety.

Courgettes have a high percentage of water and are therefore low in calories. They are a good source of Vitamin C. A versatile vegetable in the kitchen, you can even use the flowers as in the following recipe.

COURGETTE FLOWER FRITTERS
Serves 4

12 courgette flowers
125g, 5oz plain flour
2 eggs
pinch of salt
approx 150ml, ¼pt water
oil for frying

First of all remove the pistil and small green leaves from around the yellow flowers. Lightly beat the eggs with a pinch of salt and then add the flour and whisk to get rid of lumps. Stir in the water until you have a fairly liquid mixture. Set aside for 30 minutes. Dip the courgette flowers into the batter, holding them upside down to let any surplus drain off and deep fry in oil turning them over with two forks if necessary.

COURGETTES WITH DILL AND PAPRIKA
Serves 3 – 4

2 tbsp olive oil
1 onion, peeled and chopped
450g, 1lb courgettes, sliced
1 tsp dill seeds
1 tbsp hot paprika
6 tbsp soured cream

Heat the oil in a frying pan and fry the onion until soft. Add the courgettes and dill seeds. Cover and cook over a low heat until the courgettes are browned. Mix the paprika into the soured cream and stir into the courgettes. Heat through and serve.

TURKEY AND COURGETTE BURGERS
Serves 4

These are excellent healthy burgers which are a firm favourite with the children.

350g, 12oz turkey mince
4 spring onions, chopped
1 tsp chopped chives
1 courgette, grated
50g, 2oz fresh breadcrumbs
1 egg, beaten
salt and pepper
sunflower oil
3 tbsp mango chutney
4 brown baps

Put the turkey mince in a bowl with the onions, chives, grated courgette, breadcrumbs and salt and pepper. Bind together with the beaten egg and form into burger shapes. Chill for 30 minutes and then either fry in sunflower oil, or brush with oil and barbecue over hot coals. Serve in baps with mango chutney.

COURGETTE AND LEMON LINGUINI
Serves 4

4 tbsp olive oil
2 garlic cloves, peeled and chopped
1 sprig of rosemary
450g, 1lb courgettes, sliced thinly
grated rind and juice of 1 lemon
5 tbsp double cream
salt and pepper
350g, 12oz linguini
50g, 2oz walnuts, chopped

Cook the garlic and rosemary in the olive oil in a large frying pan for a couple of minutes. Leave to infuse for 5 minutes and then discard the rosemary but reserve the garlic. Cook the courgettes in the oil over a high heat until golden. Add the garlic, lemon rind, juice and cream, salt and pepper and let it all bubble for a couple of minutes, allowing the sauce to thicken a little. Cook the linguini according to the instructions on the packet and drain. Stir the linguini into the courgette mixture and add the walnuts just before serving.

COURGETTE MOUSSAKA
Serves 3 – 4

450g, 1lb courgettes
4 tbsp olive oil
450g, 1lb lean beef mince
1 onion, peeled and chopped
2 eggs
1 tsp fresh mint, chopped
400g, 14oz tin of tomatoes
1 clove of garlic, peeled and chopped
2 tbsp brown breadcrumbs
2 tbsp mature Cheddar cheese, grated

Slice the courgettes lengthways and sprinkle some salt over them. Leave them to drain for an hour. Dry them with kitchen paper and then fry in half the olive oil. Remove and add the rest of the olive oil so that you can cook the onions and mince. Fry until browned. Remove to a bowl and add the eggs and mint. Add the tinned tomatoes to the pan and garlic – allow to heat through and evaporate some of the juice. In an ovenproof dish make layers of courgette, mince and tomatoes finishing with a layer of tomato. Scatter the breadcrumbs and cheese over the top and cook in the oven at gas mark 4, 180°C (350°F) for 30 minutes.

COURGETTE AND GOAT'S CHEESE FLAN
Serves 6

225g, 8oz shortcrust pastry
450g, 1lb courgettes, sliced
15g, ½oz butter
3 eggs
225g, 8oz soft rindless goat's cheese
1 tbsp fresh chives, chopped
1 tsp fresh thyme, chopped

Roll out the pastry and use to line a greased 20cm, 8in flan dish. Bake blind in the oven at gas mark 4, 180°C (350°F) for 15 minutes. Fry the courgette slices in the butter for a few minutes to soften them. Whisk the eggs with the goat's cheese and herbs. Scatter the courgette slices over the pastry and pour the egg mixture over them. Return to the oven for another 25 minutes.

COURGETTE AND BACON BAKE
Serves 6

4 eggs
450ml, ¾pt milk
175g, 6oz mature Cheddar cheese, grated
900g, 2lb courgettes
salt, pepper and pinch of paprika
100g, 4oz streaky bacon, grilled

Beat together the eggs and milk. Stir in half the cheese and add the seasonings. Slice the courgettes and layer in a greased ovenproof dish with the bacon. Pour over the egg mixture and sprinkle with the rest of the cheese. Bake in the oven at gas mark 4, 180°C (350°F) for 40 minutes until set and golden brown.

COURGETTE GOUGÉRE
Serves 4

Choux pastry

150ml, ¼pt water
50g, 2oz butter, cut into pieces
65g, 2½oz plain flour, sieved
2 eggs, beaten
50g, 2oz Cheddar cheese, grated

Filling

2 tbsp olive oil + 25g, 1oz butter
2 onions, peeled and chopped
1 yellow pepper, deseeded and chopped
350g, 12oz courgettes, sliced
225g, 8oz tomatoes, chopped
1 tsp dried oregano
25g, 1oz mature Cheddar cheese, grated
25g, 1oz brown breadcrumbs

To make the choux pastry put the butter and water in a saucepan and heat slowly to melt the butter, then bring to the boil. Immediately add all the flour and beat until the mixture forms a ball. Cool slightly and then add the eggs a little at a time. Whisk the mixture until smooth and glossy. Stir in the cheese. Grease a 20cm, 8in flan dish and spoon the choux pastry in a circle around the dish leaving a hole in the middle. For the filling, heat the oil and butter in a frying pan and fry the onions stirring in the yellow pepper and lastly the sliced courgette. Add the tomatoes and oregano and cook for about 10 minutes. Turn this vegetable mixture into the middle of the choux pastry. Sprinkle over the cheese and breadcrumbs and bake in the oven at gas mark 5, 190°C (375°F) for 30 minutes until the choux pastry is well risen and golden.

MARROW AND TOMATO BAKE
Serves 4

450g, 1lb marrows
1 tsp salt
50g, 2oz butter
1 tbsp fresh basil, chopped
1 tbsp fresh mint, chopped
450g, 1lb tomatoes, sliced
1 large onion, peeled and chopped
300ml, ½pt white sauce
50g, 2oz mature Cheddar cheese, grated

Cut the marrows into chunks, removing the seeds and put in a colander. Sprinkle them with salt and leave to stand for 30 minutes, then rinse and dry. Use a casserole dish and put a layer of marrow chunks in the bottom. Add dots of butter, some of the basil and mint and a grinding of pepper. Lay sliced tomatoes and onion on top and add the rest of the butter, herbs and some more pepper. Stir the cheese into the white sauce. Pour over the vegetables. Cover the casserole and bake in a preheated oven at gas mark 5, 190°C (375°F) for about 45 minutes.

COURGETTE CAKE
Serves 8

The courgettes give a moist texture to the cake.

175g, 6oz courgettes, grated
120ml, 4fl oz sunflower oil
75g, 3oz light brown sugar
75g, 3oz caster sugar
2 eggs
75g, 3oz walnuts, chopped finely
100g, 4oz self-raising flour
1 tsp bicarbonate of soda
pinch of salt
½ tsp ginger
½ tsp cinnamon
pinch of nutmeg

Put the grated courgettes in a tea towel and squeeze out excess liquid. Pour the oil into a bowl and beat with the sugars. Add the eggs and continue to beat. Stir the courgette into the egg mixture with the walnuts. Sift together the flour, bicarbonate of soda, salt and spices and fold into the cake mixture. Spoon into a greased 20cm, 8in cake tin and bake in the oven at gas mark 4, 180°C (350°F) for 30 minutes.

COURGETTE, RED PEPPER AND
TOMATO CHUTNEY
Makes about 1.5kg, 3lb

8 cloves of garlic, peeled and chopped
2.5cm, 1in piece of root ginger, peeled and chopped
1 large red pepper, deseeded and chopped
900g, 2lb courgettes, sliced
900g, 2lb tomatoes, peeled and chopped
300ml, ½pt red wine vinegar
225g, 8oz granulated sugar
1 tsp salt
50g, 2oz unsalted cashew nuts, chopped
pinch of cayenne pepper

Put the garlic, ginger and red pepper in a food processor and whiz until smooth. Put this mixture with the sliced courgettes and tomatoes in a heavy saucepan and add the vinegar, sugar and salt. Stir everything together and bring to the boil. Then lower the heat, cover and simmer gently for an hour. Cook for another 30 minutes uncovered until very thick. Stir in the cashew nuts and add the cayenne pepper. Leave to cool before spooning into sterilised jars. Store in the fridge.

MARROW AND APPLE CHUTNEY
Makes about 2kg, 4lb

1 kg, 2.2lb marrow
1 tsp salt
1 kg, 2.2lb cooking apples, peeled and sliced
225g, 8oz onions, peeled and sliced
350g, 12oz brown sugar
1.2 litres, 2pts vinegar
1 tsp mustard seeds
2.5cm, 1in piece of root ginger, peeled
1 tsp peppercorns
juice of ½ a lemon

Peel and slice the marrow and cut into small pieces. Put it into a large basin layering it with some salt and leave for a few hours. Strain off any liquid that has formed. Tie the mustard seeds, ginger and peppercorns together in a piece of muslin. Put all the ingredients together in a large preserving pan, bring to boiling point and simmer gently until the mixture becomes jam-like. Remove the muslin bag, pot and seal.

CUCUMBERS

Cucumbers are one of the oldest cultivated vegetables. The first record of them was in Mesopotamia around 2000BC in the earliest known vegetable garden. There is also evidence that cucumbers were being grown in India around 1000BC. The Romans cultivated them in raised beds mounted on wheels so they could be moved around and kept in the sunshine. They were then moved under cover for the night. The Emperor Tiberius enjoyed eating them.

Columbus introduced cucumbers to the New World and records show that they were being grown by English settlers in Virginia in 1609.

If you don't have a greenhouse, cold frame or cloche then you must grow ridge cucumbers which are the hardiest forms. Burpless Tasty Green is a popular variety. These however must be sown under protection inside preferably and then can be planted outside once the danger of frosts has passed. Many people grow cucumbers from plants bought in late May or early June. They must be given plenty of water during dry weather and you should nip out the top of each shoot. They are shallow-rooted and are highly susceptible to water logging so require a water retentive soil with lots of organic matter. Planting your cucumbers in grow bags is also an option. You need to harvest them when they are about 23cm, 9in long – regular picking will encourage more fruit to form. You should, with luck, be picking a succession of cucumbers in August and September. The skin can be quite indigestible so these are best peeled. Greenhouse or indoor cucumbers are the other type of cucumber that you could grow in a cold frame if you don't have a greenhouse. Recommended varieties are Flamingo and Telegraph Improved.

Cucumbers are useful for salads, cold soups and in various hot dishes but are actually 96% water. Their flavour is in the seeds. They contain small amounts of Vitamin A and potassium.

CUCUMBER AND APPLE SOUP
Serves 4 – 6

450g, 1lb cooking apples, peeled, cored and sliced
grated rind and juice of 1 lemon
2 cucumbers, peeled
1 tsp salt
1 clove of garlic, peeled and crushed
1 glass white wine
150ml, ¼pt soured cream

Cook the apples in a little water with lemon rind and juice. Purée. Grate in the cucumber, removing any large seeds. Sprinkle with salt and leave for a couple of hours. Add the crushed garlic and wine and stir. Chill and serve with a dollop of soured cream added to each bowl of soup.

CUCUMBER AND EGG MOUSSE
Serves 6

½ a cucumber, diced
6 hard-boiled eggs
1 x 450ml, 15fl oz can jellied consommé
1 tbsp fresh majoram, chopped
300ml, ½pt double cream, whipped
sprinkling of pepper
1 tbsp fresh chives, chopped

Put the diced cucumber in a colander and sprinkle with salt. Allow to drain for an hour and then pat dry with kitchen paper. Place the eggs, consommé and majoram in a food processor and purée until smooth. Fold the whipped cream and cucumber into the egg mixture, season with pepper and add the chives. Pour the mixture into a mould or soufflé dish and chill in the fridge until set.

BACON STEAKS WITH CUCUMBER
AND APPLE SAUCE
Serves 4

4 bacon steaks
25g, 1oz butter, melted

Sauce

½ a cucumber, diced
1 eating apple, peeled, cored and diced
15g, ½oz butter
15g, ½oz flour
300ml, ½pt milk
2 tbsp double cream
1 tbsp fresh chives, chopped
pinch of cayenne pepper

Brush the bacon steaks with the melted butter and grill for 5 minutes on each side. Make the sauce by cooking the diced cucumber in boiling, salted water for 3 minutes. Drain thoroughly. Melt the butter, add the flour and stir over a low heat. Gradually pour in the milk, stirring all the time, and bring the sauce to the boil. Add seasoning and a pinch of cayenne and then the cucumber, apple, cream and chives. Stir for a couple of minutes over the heat and spoon over the bacon steaks when you serve them.

CUCUMBER WITH EGG AND LEMON SAUCE
Serves 4

1 cucumber
25g, 1oz butter
600ml, 1pt vegetable stock
salt and pepper
25g, 1oz plain flour
1 egg yolk
juice of ½ a lemon
1 tbsp fresh parsley, chopped

Peel the cucumber and cut into cubes. Place in a saucepan with the stock, salt and pepper. Simmer gently until just tender. This should only take 10 minutes. Drain and reserve the liquid. Melt the butter in a saucepan and add the flour. Stir in the cucumber cooking liquid. Mix the egg yolk and lemon juice together and whisk into the sauce. Stir in the cucumber pieces and heat gently without boiling. Sprinkle with parsley before serving.

CUCUMBER RELISH

This simple relish goes well with ham or sausages. It is also delicious served with barbecued meats. It has a sweet but tangy taste arising from the combination of hot chilli and sweetness from the sugar.

2 tbsp granulated sugar
150ml, ¼pt white wine vinegar
½ a green chilli pepper, chopped finely
1 cooking apple, cored and thinly sliced
½ a cucumber, diced

Put the sugar, vinegar and chilli pepper into a saucepan and heat gently until the sugar dissolves. Add the apple slices and bring to the boil. Boil for a couple of minutes, then add the diced cucumber and cook for a five more minutes. Serve warm or cold.

FLORENCE FENNEL

Florence fennel (known also as sweet fennel or finocchio) is different from the herb fennel. Florence fennel develops an edible bulb and comes to us from Italy. The ancient Romans and Greeks used fennel for religious and medicinal purposes as well as eating it. Soldiers ate it to keep healthy. Growing fennel in Britain can be difficult because the plant can bolt before a decent bulb forms if growth is checked by cold or drought. It is better to grow it from seed in situ as it doesn't like being transplanted. Sow in early summer 1.5cm, ½in deep and sow liberally because germination can be erratic. You can then thin plants to about 30cm, 1ft apart. You should be successful if you have a long warm, sunny summer. Fennel also needs well-drained, moisture retentive and slightly alkaline soil. When the stem base starts to develop earth up to about half the height of the bulb in order for it to blanch. and water once a week. Harvest when the bulbs are plump and eat while fresh. The leaves can also be harvested and used in salads.

Fennel is very good eaten raw and has an aniseed flavour. Alternatively you can cook it rather like celery. It goes well with white fish. Nutritionally it is a good source of potassium.

FENNEL, POTATO AND ANCHOVY SALAD
Serves 2 – 3

1 head of fennel, sliced
350g, 12oz new potatoes, cooked until just tender
60ml, 2fl oz French dressing
50g, 2oz tin of anchovies
3 hard-boiled eggs, halved
1 green pepper, deseeded and sliced
12 black olives (optional)

Put the fennel and potatoes in a bowl and pour the French dressing over them. Drain the anchovies and add to the salad along with the eggs, green pepper and olives.

BRAISED FENNEL
Serves 4

2 heads of fennel, quartered
25g, 1oz butter
150ml, ¼pt vegetable stock
1 tbsp lemon juice
salt and pepper
2 tbsp Parmesan cheese, grated

Melt the butter in a large saucepan and cook the fennel for several minutes. Add the stock, lemon juice, salt and pepper. Cover and simmer for 30 minutes. Transfer to a serving dish, sprinkle with the cheese and brown under a hot grill before serving.

MEDITERRANEAN FISH
AND FENNEL CASSEROLE
Serves 4

2 tbsp olive oil
2 cloves of garlic, peeled and chopped
175g, 6oz mushrooms, chopped
225g, 8oz tomatoes, chopped
2 heads of fennel, quartered
300ml, ½pt chicken stock
225g, 8oz white fish such as cod fillet
salt and pepper
1 tbsp tomato purée
1 tsp mustard
1 tbsp double cream
1 tbsp fresh parsley, chopped
1 tbsp fresh chives, chopped

Heat the oil in a large frying pan and add the garlic, mushrooms and tomatoes. Then add the fennel and cook over a low heat for several minutes. Add the stock and fish, cut into cubes. Season with salt and pepper and simmer for 15 minutes. Add the tomato purée, mustard and cream and blend together. Transfer to a serving dish and sprinkle with the herbs before serving.

FRENCH AND RUNNER BEANS

It is thought that French beans originated in Peru around 8000BC and from there the vegetable spread throughout South and Central America. These beans were not introduced into Europe until the sixteenth century when Spanish explorers brought them from their voyages to the New World. They were called kidney beans at first, alluding to the shape of the seeds. They became known as French beans in Britain simply because they were imported from France but are also known as dwarf beans or haricots verts. In the early days only the seeds were eaten and they were known as flageolots or dried as haricots. Nowadays the ripe seeds are of course still eaten as kidney, haricot, flageolot or borlotti beans either dried or cooked and canned. Runner beans originated in Mexico around 1000 BC and when first introduced to Britain in the 1600s were used as ornamental climbers. It wasn't until the eighteenth century that the British realised the pods were edible.

Runner beans are of course very similar to French beans, the difference being they have larger, coarser and stronger flavoured pods. They are very easy to grow but now there are so many varieties of climbing French beans on the market that we are rather spoilt for choice with yellow and purple-podded varieties as well as green. Standard climbing varieties of French beans should be sown 5cm, 2in deep in rows 23cm, 9in apart. Dwarf varieties can be sown 15cm, 6in apart in rows 60cm, 2ft apart. None of these varieties should be sown until the danger of frost is past, at the end of May or beginning of June. Dwarf beans can be sown up until early July. Runner beans benefit from well manured ground. French beans need phosphate rich soil so it is a good idea to supply a pinch of superphosphate in each planting hole 5cm, 2in below the seeds. Climbing French beans and Runner beans need to grow up canes. Beans in general need little water during the early stages but watering twice a week at flowering time and when the pods are forming will increase the yield. Good dwarf French bean varieties are Royalty (purple-podded), Sungold and Mont d'Or (yellow podded) and Tendergreen which is a traditional stringless green-podded variety. Recommended climbing varieties are Blue Lake, Eva, Meraviglia di Venezia (golden podded), and Cosse Violette (purple-podded). I have grown the Meraviglia di Venezia which crop very heavily but late on in the year in October – the danger is that the plants can be ruined by frost before you have finished harvesting the beans. The most popular variety of runner beans is Scarlet Emperor which has, as the name suggests, scarlet flowers. In general you should be harvesting your beans in September - if you harvest regularly you will encourage the production of more flowers. You could also try growing borlotti beans which are the Italian version of French beans. Plant the climbing variety Lingua di Fuoco. The pods are a striking green with red stripes. This is a dual purpose bean - you can pick and eat the whole pods when young or harvest the whole plant in mid autumn and dry on newspaper; then pod the beans.

Pests that may affect your beans are Bean Seed Fly which damage the seedlings and Black Bean Aphid attack French beans as well as broad beans (see page 20).

Green beans are an excellent source of vitamins K, A and C and potassium. They are also a good source of fibre.

Stakes
for your
runner
beans.

SALADE NIÇOISE
Serves 6

Handful of salad leaves
175g, 6oz French beans
½ a cucumber, cut into sticks
1 red onion, peeled and sliced thinly
4 eggs, hard-boiled
185g, 7oz tin of tuna steaks in oil, drained
handful of cherry tomatoes, halved
50g, 2oz tin of anchovies
50g, 2oz black olives, halved

Dressing

5 tbsp olive oil
1 tbsp balsamic vinegar
1 clove of garlic, peeled and crushed
salt and pepper

First cook the French beans in boiling water for 3 or 4 minutes, drain and put under cold running water to retain their green colour. Arrange the salad leaves in a bowl and spread the beans, onion and cucumber over them. Halve the boiled eggs and add to the salad along with the tuna, tomatoes, anchovies and olives. For the dressing stir together the oil, vinegar, garlic and salt and pepper and pour over the salad.

FRENCH BEAN PURÉE
Serves 3 – 4

450g, 1lb French beans, topped, tailed and cooked
sprig of savory
salt and pepper
25g, 1oz butter
1 tbsp lemon juice + a little grated lemon peel

Purée the beans with the savory and seasoning until smooth. Heat the butter until brown and add the grated lemon peel and lemon juice. Mix in the bean purée and serve at once.

SAUTÉED FRENCH BEANS WITH RED PEPPER
Serves 3 – 4   - see photo in colour section

450g, 1lb French beans, topped and tailed
2 tbsp olive oil
15g, ½oz butter
1 red pepper, deseeded and sliced
2 spring onions, sliced
1 tbsp sunflower seeds, roasted

Bring a pan of water to the boil and add the beans. Cook them for 3 or 4 minutes and then drain and refresh under cold water. Heat the oil and butter in a large frying pan and add the red pepper. Cook for a couple of minutes and then add the French beans and spring onions. Sauté for a few minutes. Sprinkle with sunflower seeds and serve.

FRENCH BEANS
WITH MUSHROOM CREAM SAUCE
Serves 4

450g, 1lb French beans, topped and tailed
50g, 2oz butter

1 onion, peeled and chopped
100g, 4oz mushrooms, sliced
squeeze of lemon juice
6 tbsp single cream

Cook the beans in boiling water until just tender and drain them. Melt the butter in a frying pan and fry the onion gently until soft. Add the mushrooms and squeeze a little lemon juice over them. Cook for 5 minutes. Mix the beans with the onion and mushrooms and stir in the cream. Simmer over a low heat for 3 minutes by which time the sauce should have thickened. Serve as a side dish.

FRENCH BEANS WITH PEARS
Serves 4

This is a German idea and goes well with pork, making a change from the more usual apple sauce.

450g, 1lb French beans, topped and tailed
3 pears, peeled and sliced
25g, 1oz butter
25g, 1oz flour
300ml, ½pt stock from boiling the beans and pears
1 tbsp lemon juice
pinch of sugar

Bring a pan of salted water to the boil and add the beans and the pears. Cook until the pears have softened. Drain and reserve the stock. Melt the butter in a small saucepan and stir in the flour. Gradually add the reserved stock and stir over a low heat until you have a smooth sauce. Stir in the lemon juice and sugar. Pour over the beans and pears and serve at once.

BORLOTTI BEAN AND TUNA PASTA SALAD
Serves 4 – 5

You will need to soak your borlotti beans overnight in water with a spoonful of bicarbonate of soda. Drain well, rinse and cook them in water, simmering gently for about an hour.

450g, 1lb pasta shapes, cooked
4 tbsp olive oil + 1 tbsp lemon juice
350g, 12oz borlotti beans
185g, 7oz tin of tuna, drained
1 red pepper, deseeded and diced
4 spring onions, chopped
1 tbsp fresh parsley, chopped

Put the pasta in a serving bowl and drizzle with the olive oil and lemon juice. Add the beans, tuna, red pepper and onions. Sprinkle with parsley and serve.

BORLOTTI BEAN AND AUBERGINE DIP

1 aubergine, cooked in the oven until soft
350g, 12oz borlotti beans
2 cloves of garlic, peeled and crushed
1 tsp ground cumin
1 tsp ground coriander
1 tsp tahini
juice of ½ a lemon

Scoop out the flesh of the aubergine and purée all the ingredients in a food processor until smooth.

RUNNER BEANS À LA GRECQUE
Serves 4 – 6

450g, 1lb runner beans, stringed and sliced into strips
1 tsp salt

1 onion, peeled and chopped
3 tomatoes, blanched, peeled and chopped
4 tbsp fresh parsley, chopped
2 tbsp olive oil
2 tsp sugar
sprinkling of pepper

Put the beans into a colander and sprinkle them with salt. Leave for about an hour to soften. Rinse and dry the beans and then combine with the onion, tomatoes, parsley and olive oil in a saucepan. Sprinkle with sugar and add some pepper. Add just enough boiling water to cover, probably about 300ml, ½pt and bring to simmering point. Half cover the pan and cook gently for 30 minutes by which time the sauce should be thick. If it is too thick add a little more water. Serve warm or cold.

RUNNER BEANS AU GRATIN
Serves 4

450g, 1lb runner beans
15g, ½oz butter
1 red onion, peeled and sliced
1 tbsp plain flour
300ml, ½pt milk
2 tbsp brown breadcrumbs
50g, 2oz mature Cheddar cheese, grated

Cook the runner beans in boiling salted water for a few minutes. Melt the butter in a small saucepan and add the onion. Cook until softened, then stir in the flour and gradually add the milk, stirring until you have a smooth sauce. Transfer the runner beans to an ovenproof dish and pour the onion sauce over them. Sprinkle with the breadcrumbs and cheese and cook in the oven for 20 minutes at gas mark 4, 180°C (350°F) until golden and bubbling on top.

JERUSALEM ARTICHOKES

Jerusalem artichokes have nothing to do with Jerusalem nor with globe artichokes but it is thought that the word is a corruption of the Italian word Girasole, meaning sunflower and literally 'turning in the sun'. They are related to sunflowers and grow in a similar way. These root tubers originated in North America, or more exactly in Nova Scotia where the French found them growing in the seventeenth century. The French brought them back to Europe and the Dutch grew them extensively before exporting them to Britain. They are not that popular in this country – it was realised as long ago as 1622 that they can cause wind – Dr Venner of Bath wrote: 'It breedeth melancholy and is somewhat nauseous and fulsome to the stomach,' and John Goodyer who grew them in Hampshire wrote of the artichoke: 'In my judgement they stir and cause a filthy loathsome sticking wind within the body thereby causing the belly to be pained and tormented and are a meat more fit for swine than man.' As a result of their effect on the digestive system they have been nicknamed 'fartichokes'. They are also very knobbly and difficult to peel which may put some people off growing them but they are a useful vegetable to have in the winter.

Artichokes are incredibly easy to grow and rather like mint seem to grow back every year because invariably one fails to dig up every tuber and the ones left in the ground grow again in the spring. Like sunflowers, Jerusalem artichokes grow very tall, to about 3metres, 10 feet but their leaves are smaller and they only actually flower in very hot summers.

Artichokes are grown from tubers which can be purchased from seed suppliers/Garden Centres or from tubers saved from the year before. They will grow in almost any soil but well-manured clay soils produce the heaviest crops. Tubers should be planted in February about 8cm, 3in deep in the soil and should be at least 30cm, 1ft apart with about 90cm, 3ft between rows. They only need watering if it is very dry in August and this should enhance the yield. Once they have reached their full height their stalks may easily be blown over in the wind but you can cut them back in the autumn without damaging the tubers which should be harvested whenever you require them from November onwards.

Artichokes contain inulin which promotes good bacteria and detoxes the colon - they are low in calories and have moderate amounts of Vitamins B1 and 5. They have a distinct, unusual flavour similar to water chestnuts. After peeling, sprinkle with lemon juice to prevent them going brown or put into a bowl of water to which you have added a little vinegar. If eaten with leafy vegetables or with crusty rolls they are apparently less likely to cause wind. They work very well in soup - here are two versions.

ARTICHOKE AND BRUSSELS SPROUT SOUP
Serves 4

3 tbsp olive oil
1 medium onion, peeled and sliced
450g, 1lb Jerusalem artichokes, peeled and sliced
900ml, 1½pts vegetable stock
225g, 8oz Brussels sprouts, trimmed and sliced
4 tbsp single cream
2 tbsp hazelnuts, chopped
1 tbsp fresh parsley, chopped

Sauté the onion in the olive oil in a large saucepan. Add the artichokes and cook for several minutes. Pour in the stock. Bring to the boil and then cover, turn down the heat and simmer for 25 minutes, stirring every so often. Add the sprouts and cook for another 5 minutes. Purée the mixture in a liquidizer or food processor, reheat and stir in the cream and sprinkle each portion with hazelnuts and parsley before serving.

ARTICHOKE AND BUTTERNUT SQUASH SOUP
Serves 4

3 tbsp olive oil
1 medium onion, peeled and sliced
450g, 1lb Jerusalem artichokes, peeled and sliced
225g, 8oz butternut squash, peeled and diced
900ml, 1½pts vegetable stock
1 tsp fresh thyme, chopped
2 tbsp crème fraîche
1 tbsp fresh parsley, chopped

Sauté the onion in the olive oil in large saucepan. Add the artichokes and allow to cook for several minutes. Mix in the squash and after a couple of minutes pour in the stock. Bring to the boil and then cover and allow to simmer for 30 minutes, stirring every so often. Purée the mixture in a liquidizer or food processor. Reheat and add a dollop of crème fraîche and some parsley into each bowl of soup before serving.

ARTICHOKE AND POTATO CROQUETTES
Serves 4

225g, 8oz potatoes, peeled and boiled
225g, 8oz Jerusalem artichokes, peeled, sliced and cooked
2 tbsp flour + 1 beaten egg for coating
breadcrumbs mixed with some finely chopped Brazil nuts

Purée together the potato and artichoke. Form the mixture into sausage shapes and dip first in some flour, then in beaten egg and then in the breadcrumbs and nuts. Fry in batches in a deep fat fryer or deep frying pan filled at least 2.5cm, 1in with oil.

ARTICHOKES WITH THICK TOMATO SAUCE
Serves 4 – 6

1 onion, peeled and sliced
1 clove of garlic, peeled and crushed
3 tbsp olive oil
450g, 1lb Jerusalem artichokes, peeled and sliced
400g, 14oz tin of tomatoes
1 tbsp tomato purée
1 tbsp fresh parsley, chopped

Fry the onion and garlic in the olive oil in a large frying pan until softened. Add the artichokes and cook for 5 minutes. Tip the tin of tomatoes and the purée into the pan, stir and cook covered for 25 minutes. Add the parsley and serve. The artichokes should still have a bit of a crunch to them.

ARTICHOKES AU GRATIN
Serves 3 – 4

450g, 1lb Jerusalem artichokes, scrubbed
15g, ½oz butter
1 tbsp flour
300ml, ½pt milk
2 egg yolks
½ tsp mustard powder
75g, 3oz mature Cheddar cheese, grated
25g, 1oz brown breadcrumbs

Put the artichokes into a saucepan of boiling, salted water and boil for 10 to 15 minutes or until tender. Slice them up and layer in a greased ovenproof dish. Make the sauce by melting the butter, add the flour and then gradually add the milk to make a white sauce. Stir in the egg yolks, mustard powder and half the cheese. Pour over the artichokes and sprinkle the rest of the cheese and breadcrumbs over the top. Bake in the oven at gas mark 4, 180°C (350°F) for 15 minutes and serve immediately.

KALE

The word kale is derived from the Latin word 'caulis'. It is related to cabbage but does not form a heart. There are many different varieties but Borecole is merely a particular variety and not another name for kale as some catalogues/books maintain. Borecole was a type of kale that was the staple food of Dutch Peasants or Boers, hence Boers' kale (Boerenkool). Kale has long been cultivated in northern Europe but the Scots are perhaps the keenest kale eaters and their kale brose (a kale and oatmeal soup) used to form part of their staple diet.

Kale is extremely hardy, withstanding very low temperatures and therefore is not killed off by frosts. It is a really useful vegetable to grow for winter use as the fresh young leaves can be used in salads. Russian Kale and Hungry Gap are the hardiest types.

Kale does well on ground previously used for a potato crop so you could easily grow some after you have harvested early potatoes in June. It can be planted from March under cloches if you want to use the baby leaves in salads and they will be ready 8 – 12 weeks from sowing. Red Russian Kale is good for this. Otherwise plant seeds outside from April to June in 12mm, ½in drills and you should be able to harvest your kale from November through the winter. Rows should be 30cm, 1ft apart. Nero di Toscana (also known as Black Tuscany or Cavolo Nero) produces an excellent crop and Red Winter produces red frilly leaves on purple stems so is very attractive. Redbor is another red variety for picking through the winter and young leaves can also be used in salads. Hungry Gap is a late variety which you can plant in July for harvesting the following spring. I have tried Pentland Brig which lasted well through the winter, producing green curly-edged leaves.

Kale is rich in iron, Vitamin C and calcium. Pick mainly the young leaves as older leaves can be bitter. If picked regularly you should get a good supply over a number of weeks.

CURLY KALE SOUP
Serves 4 – 6

1½ litres, 3pts vegetable stock
50g, 2oz oatmeal
450g, 1lb curly kale
salt and pepper

Bring the stock to the boil and add the oatmeal. Leave to simmer gently while you shred the kale. Add the kale to the stock along with salt and pepper and simmer for 20 minutes, uncovered.

COLCANNON WITH KALE
Serves 4

A traditional Irish dish made with cabbage or kale but nowadays with many variations.

450g, 1lb potatoes, peeled and cooked
50g, 2oz butter
salt and pepper
1 leek, sliced
90ml, 3fl oz milk
225g, 8oz curly kale

Mash the potato with half the butter, adding salt and pepper to taste. Cook the leek in the milk for 5 minutes and then stir into the mashed potato. Steam the kale for no more than 5 minutes, chop it up and mix into the potato over a low heat. Spoon into a serving dish. Make a well in the centre and fill with the remaining butter. Serve at once.

STIR FRIED KALE WITH BRUSSELS SPROUTS
Serves 3 – 4

2 tbsp olive oil
225g, 8oz curly kale, cut into strips
100g, 4oz Brussels sprouts, trimmed and shredded
1 tbsp pine nuts

Heat the oil in a wok. Throw in the kale and sprouts and cook without allowing to brown for a couple of minutes. Add the pine nuts and heat for another minute. Serve immediately.

ORIENTAL-STYLE STIR FRIED KALE
Serves 4

1 tbsp sesame oil
1 small piece root ginger, peeled and grated
2 cloves of garlic, peeled and chopped
450g, 1lb curly kale, shredded
1 onion, peeled and thinly sliced
3 tbsp soya sauce
3 tbsp sherry
1 tbsp sesame seeds

Heat the sesame oil in a wok and add the ginger and garlic. After 30 seconds add the kale and onion. Stir fry for a couple of minutes and then add the soya sauce and sherry. Bring to the boil and serve immediately sprinkled with sesame seeds.

KALE AND CARROT AU GRATIN
Serves 4 – 6

This makes a good hearty vegetarian meal or could accompany plainly cooked white fish.

300ml, ½pt vegetable stock
1 onion, peeled and chopped
1 tsp fresh thyme, chopped
75g, 3oz long grain rice
2 large carrots, peeled and sliced
1kg, 2.2lb curly kale
100g, 4oz ricotta
75g, 3oz mature Cheddar cheese, grated
pinch of nutmeg
salt and pepper
2 tbsp wholemeal breadcrumbs

Heat the stock in a saucepan with the onion and thyme and bring to the boil. Add the rice and simmer until the rice is cooked. This should take about 15 minutes. Add the sliced carrots about 5 minutes before the end of the cooking time. Steam the kale for no more than 3 or 4 minutes. Transfer the rice to an ovenproof dish and mix in the kale, ricotta and half the cheese. Sprinkle the breadcrumbs and the remaining cheese on top and dribble with olive oil. Cook in the oven at gas mark 4, 180°C (350°F) for about 20 minutes and finish browning the top under the grill if necessary.

LEEKS

'Eat leeks in March and wild garlic in May and all year after physicians may play'.

Leeks were cultivated by the ancient Egyptians. The Greeks ate them and Hippocrates believed that leeks were a cure for nosebleeds. The Romans were keen growers of leeks; the Emperor Nero, in particular, was enthusiastic about eating them, saying they helped clear his voice. Roman legions brought the leek to Wales and it soon became the national emblem. To celebrate a famous battle victory in which King Cadwallader beat the Saxons in AD640, Welsh soldiers wore leeks in their hats. As a result March 1st is celebrated as St David's Day and the Welsh still wear leeks in their hats.

Leeks are easy to grow as they are very hardy but they need a long season to mature. Sowing seeds at intervals can result in your leeks being harvested from early autumn to late spring. Leeks hate acid soil but need deep soil with plenty of well-rotted manure dug in. Sow seeds in the middle of March in shallow drills about 2.5cm, 1in apart and then in July transfer the seedlings to their final position by which time they should be about 15cm, 6in high. Space the plants 23cm, 9in apart and make deep holes of about 23cm, 9in – put the plants in these holes as deep as the base of the leaves but do not fill the soil back in again round the plants. Instead pour water into the holes – this will wash some soil into the bottom of the hole. This method of growing leeks is necessary for the blanching of the stems and it allows less earth to fall down between the leaves. Water once a week until the plants are well established but after that only if there is a drought. Early varieties (King Richard is recommended) are ready for harvesting in autumn but late varieties, such as Natan, will keep you in leeks until mid spring. Musselburgh is an old established variety which is very winter hardy and will be ready for cropping from December onwards.

When preparing leeks for cooking, be really careful to remove all the dirt which is often hidden behind the outer leaves. The Scots were great lovers of leeks and invented the famous soup: cock-a-leekie. Leeks are rich in potassium, iron and vitamins B and C.

LEEK AND POTATO SOUP
Serves 2 – 3

3 leeks, washed
3 tbsp olive oil
3 potatoes, peeled
25g, 1oz butter
2 tbsp single cream
600ml, 1pt milk

Slice the leeks and fry in olive oil. Chop up the potatoes and add to the leeks with the butter. Cook for a couple of minutes turning the potatoes in the butter. Transfer to a saucepan and add the milk. Cook over a moderate heat for about 20 minutes. Purée the mixture and return to the pan. Reheat and stir in the cream before serving.

LEEK PURÉE WITH BUTTER
AND A TOUCH OF CREAM
Serves 4 – 6

1kg, 2.2lb leeks, washed
50g, 2oz butter
2 tbsp double cream
salt and pepper

Slice the leeks but only use the white part. The green part tends to be too strong when only lightly cooked. Fry in half the butter for 5 minutes. Then purée in the food processor with the rest of the butter and double cream. Add salt and pepper to taste.

LEEK AND TOMATO TART
Serves 4 – 6

Spiced cheese pastry

50g, 2oz butter
50g, 2oz mature Cheddar cheese, grated
pinch of chilli powder
1 egg
75g, 3oz plain flour

Filling

4 tomatoes
1 large leek
25g, 1oz butter
3 eggs
150ml, ¼pt single cream
1 tbsp parsley, chopped
2 tbsp tomato purée

To make the pastry beat together the butter and cheese, chilli powder and egg. Add the flour and stir together. Knead until smooth and then wrap in clingfilm and chill for about 15 minutes. Roll out and use to line a greased 20cm, 8in flan tin. Bake blind in the oven at gas mark 4, 180°C (350°F) for 10 minutes. Meanwhile plunge the tomatoes into boiling water for a minute so that you can then skin them. Cut them in half and slice the leeks thinly. Melt the butter in a saucepan and add the tomatoes and leeks. Cook over a low heat until softened. Then arrange the leeks and tomato over the pastry base. Whisk together the eggs and cream and stir in the tomato purée and parsley. Pour over the tomato and leek mixture. Return to the oven for another 25 minutes.

LEEKS WITH BACON AND CHEESE
Serves 6

6 leeks, washed and trimmed
6 rashers unsmoked back bacon
75g, 3oz mature Cheddar cheese, grated

Wrap a rasher of bacon around each leek. Lay leeks in an oiled ovenproof dish and cook for 20 minutes. Sprinkle the cheese over the leeks and bacon and finish under the grill.

TUNA AND LEEK PASTA
Serves 3 – 4

1 leek, washed and sliced
1 red pepper, deseeded and chopped
1 tbsp olive oil
185g, 7oz tin of tuna in oil, drained
grated peel and juice from 1 lime
200ml, 7fl oz tub of crème fraîche
350g, 12oz pasta shapes, such as farfalle
black pepper

Fry the leek and red pepper in the oil until softened. Stir in the tuna, lime juice and zest and the crème fraîche. Keep warm. Cook the pasta in a saucepan of salted boiling water according to the packet instructions. Drain and stir the pasta into the tuna and leek mixture. Grind some black pepper over the dish and serve hot.

TURKEY MEATBALLS WITH LEEKS
Serves 4

Serve these meatballs with brown rice.

450g, 1lb turkey mince
1 slice of brown bread
1 egg
1 tsp fresh thyme, chopped
2 tbsp olive oil
450g, 1lb leeks, washed
1 clove of garlic, peeled and crushed
400g, 14oz tin of chopped tomatoes
2 tbsp tomato purée

Make up the meatballs by processing the bread, mince, egg and thyme. Divide into about 16 and roll into balls. Fry the meatballs in the olive oil. Slice the leeks into ribbons. Add the garlic and leeks to the frying pan. Then stir in the tomatoes and tomato purée. Cook covered for about 15 minutes, adding a little water if the mixture becomes too dry.

LEEK AND GOAT'S CHEESE TORTILLA
Serves 3 – 4

2 tbsp olive oil
2 leeks, washed and sliced
1 red pepper, deseeded and sliced
4 eggs
3 tbsp single cream
4 thick slices of goat's cheese
1 tbsp fresh parsley, chopped

Heat the oil in a large frying pan and cook the leeks and red pepper until softened. Beat the eggs with the cream and pour on to the leeks and pepper. Cook until the egg is almost set and browning on the bottom. Add the slices of goat's cheese and finish off under a preheated grill. Serve at once garnished with parsley.

LEEK AND MUSHROOM CROUSTADE
Serves 4 – 6

75g, 3oz breadcrumbs
75g, 3oz flaked almonds
75g,3oz ground almonds
1 small onion, peeled and grated
75g, 3oz butter
225g, 8oz leeks, washed and sliced
225g, 8oz mushrooms, sliced
180ml, 6fl oz Greek yoghurt
pinch of nutmeg

Mix together the breadcrumbs, flaked and ground almonds, onion and melted butter. The mixture should bind together like crumbly pastry. Press into a greased 20cm, 8in flan dish and bake in the oven at gas mark 4, 180°C (350°F) for 20 minutes until crisp and golden. Fry the mushrooms and leeks in butter for about 10 minutes until all the liquid has evaporated. Spoon the mushrooms and leeks on top of the croustade. Swirl the Greek yoghurt over the top of the vegetables and sprinkle a little nutmeg over the top. Return to the oven to heat through for 5 minutes.

LEEK, TOMATO AND PESTO BAKE
Serves 2 – 3

2 leeks, washed and trimmed
8 cherry tomatoes, halved
2 tbsp green pesto sauce
2 tbsp fromage frais
50g, 2oz mature Cheddar cheese, grated

Cut the leeks into large chunks and surround with the cherry tomatoes in an ovenproof dish. Mix together the pesto sauce and fromage frais and spoon over the leek and tomato. Sprinkle the cheese on top. Bake in the oven at gas mark 4, 180°C (350°F) for 25 minutes. Serve with crusty bread.

LETTUCE AND ROCKET

Lettuce has a long and fascinating history dating back to 6000BC in Egypt where there is evidence on wall paintings that the Egyptians ate lettuce. Darius, King of Persia, certainly served lettuce around 500BC. The Greeks and Romans cultivated a cos-type lettuce. The Cos lettuce derives its name from the island of Cos but no one is sure whether it was developed when the Ptolemies were ruling Cos or later by the Romans after they had defeated Cleopatra on Cos. The word lactuca (the Latin term for lettuce) refers to the milky, lactic sap that you can see when you cut a lettuce. The Romans believed this sap had medicinal properties. It is in fact highly narcotic and can be used as a substitute for opium. The Greeks valued lettuces because of their soporific effect. The Romans are thought to have introduced lettuce to Britain. Nothing much is known about the use of lettuce after that until the 1600s when there is evidence that Cos lettuce was being eaten – John Evelyn mentioned it in his Salad Calendar. Christopher Columbus introduced it to America.

There are four types of lettuce: Loose Leaf, Butterhead, Cos and Crisphead. The Loose Leaf are the type that do not form hearts and there are now many varieties of these which are also known as 'cut and come again' - if you pick a few leaves from each plant new ones will form in their place. Butterhead types form a heart but the leaves are soft and delicate. The Cos lettuce forms an upright, elongated heart and takes longer to mature than other types – it is used to make a Caesar salad. The Crisphead, of which the Iceberg and Webb's Wonderful are the best known varieties, takes on the appearance of a cabbage with succulent, crisp and wrinkled leaves. These however tend to be less nutritious with their pale green leaves.

There are so many varieties of lettuce available now that if you plant carefully you can have some type of lettuce growing in your garden all year round. You can start planting seed under cloches in February and you should be eating salad leaves in April/May. You can plant different seeds all through the summer and there are types for autumn sowing such as Winter Density and Rouge d'Hiver which will survive the winter without protection. There are many different coloured lettuces from pale to dark green to green-speckled with red to red-tinted to almost completely crimson. Red Salad Bowl, Lollo Rossa, Amorina and New Red Fire are all red, easy to grow cut-and-come-again lettuces, popular with the children (leaves tend to lose their colour as temperatures rise but become redder in the autumn).

Rocket has been cultivated since Roman times. It was popular in Elizabethan England but has only regained its popularity in the last decade or so. It is ever popular in Italy where it is sold in big bunches at market stalls. It is very easy to grow, germinating in reasonably low temperatures. The younger leaves are milder and it is best to harvest regularly to prevent the plants bolting. It does run to seed in the summer, preferring cooler temperatures. The flowers are edible and could be added to salads. In seed catalogues it is also known as Roquette or Rucola. Wild rocket is a different species which is more peppery than ordinary rocket but also worth trying.

You will definitely encounter problems with slugs who like eating all salad type leaves and if you don't want to use slug pellets, you can put out beer traps – containers filled with beer which the slugs will be attracted to.

The greener the leaves, as a rule the more nutritious the lettuce, providing more beta-carotene. Lettuces are a good source of folate. They are however 95% water. Rocket is high in potassium and vitamin C. I have only included here some more unusual lettuce recipes – I am sure you all know how to make salads and there is nothing nicer than using all the different salad leaves you have grown in a simple salad with olive oil, balsamic vinegar and some Maldon sea salt. You are sure to have a glut of lettuces in the summer so I have included 3 soups.

LETTUCE AND AVOCADO SOUP
Serves 4

900ml, 1½pts vegetable stock
2 lettuces, washed and chopped
2 avocados, stoned and peeled
60ml. 2fl oz dry white wine
1 green chilli, seeded and chopped
150ml, ¼pt soured cream

Bring the stock to the boil in a large saucepan, add the lettuces and turn off the heat. Leave for 2 minutes, then remove the lettuces and allow the stock to cool. Mash the avocados and add the wine and chilli. Add the lettuces and the cool stock. Blend in a liquidizer or food processor, stir in the soured cream and serve.

LETTUCE AND SPINACH SOUP
Serves 6

1 lettuce, washed
a few spinach leaves
2 small leeks
450g, 1lb peas
50g, 2oz butter
1.2 litres, 2pts vegetable stock
4 slices of bread, diced
2 tbsp olive oil
3 tbsp crème fraîche

Shred the lettuce, and spinach. Slice the leeks. Put the lettuce, spinach, leeks and peas in a saucepan with the butter. Add a little of the stock. Simmer, covered for 15 minutes. Add the remaining stock and bring back to the boil. Purée the vegetables and reheat.

In the meantime make the croutons by frying the bread in the olive oil in a frying pan until crisp. Serve with a dollop of crème fraîche on each portion and some croutons.

CREAMED LETTUCE AND CUCUMBER SOUP
Serves 2 – 3

1 lettuce, washed
50g, 2oz butter
½ a cucumber, sliced
1 onion, peeled and chopped
50g, 2oz peas
300ml, ½pt vegetable stock
300ml, ½pt milk
2 egg yolks
4 tbsp single cream
1 tbsp chives, chopped

Separate the leaves of the lettuce. Melt the butter in a saucepan and add the leaves with the cucumber and onion. Cook for 15 minutes until the vegetables have absorbed the butter. Blanch the peas for a couple of minutes in boiling water and then drain and add to the lettuce mixture. Add the stock and milk and cook for a few more minutes. Purée the soup and return to the pan. Beat the egg yolks with the cream and mix with a little of the soup, before pouring into the pan. Reheat gently and add the chives.

BRAISED LETTUCE WITH CARROTS
Serves 3 – 4

1 lettuce, Iceberg if possible
1 carrot, peeled
1 small onion, peeled
25g, 1oz butter
2 tbsp vegetable stock
1 egg yolk
1 tbsp cream

Cut the lettuce into quarters and place cut sides down in a small casserole. Slice the carrot thinly along with the onion and scatter over the lettuce. Dot with butter and add the stock. Cover and cook for 10 minutes. Stir in the egg yolk and cream and serve at once.

CAESAR SALAD
Serves 6

2 Cos lettuces
6 anchovy fillets
2 cloves of garlic, peeled and crushed
½ tsp English mustard
few drops of Worcestershire sauce
50g, 2oz croutons
juice of 1 lemon
2 egg yolks
50g, 2oz Parmesan cheese, grated
150ml, ¼pt olive oil

Tear the Cos into bite-sized pieces. Put the anchovies, garlic, mustard and Worcestershire sauce in a large bowl and add a few croutons. Mash the ingredients to a thick, smooth paste. Add lemon juice and egg yolks and stir together. Add half the Parmesan and pour in the oil in a thin stream beating the dressing as you go. Toss in the lettuce and the remaining croutons and Parmesan.

ROCKET SALSA
Serves 4

This goes well with white fish, chicken or lamb.

1 clove of garlic, peeled and crushed
1 onion, peeled and chopped
1 tbsp fresh parsley
2 handfuls of rocket
juice of ½ a lemon
200ml, 7fl oz olive oil

All the ingredients can be processed together in a food processor. Start with processing the onion and garlic, then add the parsley and rocket and lastly the lemon juice and olive oil. Do not over process as you want the mixture to have some texture to it.

LENTIL, ROCKET AND SORREL TART
Serves 6

225g, 8oz shortcrust pastry
75g, 3oz puy lentils, cooked
1 tbsp olive oil
1 onion, peeled and chopped
knob of butter
handful of rocket + 6 sorrel leaves, chopped
3 eggs
300ml, ½pt single cream
100g, 4oz mature Cheddar cheese, grated

Roll out the pastry and use to line a greased 20cm, 8in flan tin. Prick the base and bake blind in the oven at gas mark 4, 180°C (350°F) for 10 minutes. Mix the cooked puy lentils with the olive oil. Fry the onion in a little butter, add the rocket and sorrel and cook until they wilt. Mix with the lentils and spread over the pastry. Whisk together the eggs and cream and pour over the lentil mixture.Sprinkle the cheese over the top. Return to the oven for 25 minutes until risen and golden brown.

ONIONS

Onions are one of the oldest vegetables probably cultivated 5,000 years ago. They grew wild in various regions and they were an ideal vegetable to cultivate since they were easy to grow, transportable, kept well and could be grown in a variety of soils and climates. Onions may well have originated in Central Asia. The ancient Egyptians used them extensively, fed them to their slaves working on the Pyramids and buried them with the Pharaohs. The onion with its spherical shape and concentric rings symbolized eternity and was regarded as a sacred object, almost a God, to be called upon when swearing a solemn oath. Onions have frequently been found in Mummies stuffed in the pelvic regions, the thorax, flattened against the ears and in the eye sockets. Presumably the Egyptians believed the onion had antiseptic qualities which could be useful in the afterlife. The Romans were keen on onions - Pliny wrote of Pompeii's onions and cabbages - excavators at Pompeii indeed found evidence that onions had grown there. The Romans believed the onion could cure vision, induce sleep, heal mouth sores and cure toothache. Gladiators were rubbed down with onion juice to firm up their muscles. The Romans probably brought onions over to England. However it wasn't until the Middle Ages that they gained popularity in Britain.

Shallots have an interesting history – apparently the word Shallot comes from eschalot, a corruption of the word Ascalon, a place in Syria where in 1192 Richard I defeated the armies of Saladin and it is believed he and the Crusaders brought this small onion back to England.

Onions are technically biennials - they store food in their bulbs during the first growing season and flower in their second season. Their leaves are of course edible as spring onions.

Onions are easiest to grow as sets and planted out in March. A good variety of red onion, Red Baron, is definitely worth growing. Shallots are a satisfying onion to grow (particularly because they are expensive in the shops) which you can also buy as sets – Golden Gourmet are an easily available variety which are high yielding and store well. Pickling onions are grown from seed and should be planted 1cm, ½in apart. Salad (spring) onion varieties are now available in the seed catalogues that you can grow from seed planting out from April to August. The North Holland variety produces red/purple stems so are unusual and attractive.

Onions should be grown in the same area only one year in three. The soil should be high in organic matter, preferably with well rotted manure dug into the soil the autumn before. They like free-draining soil and do not do well on heavy clay soil. Otherwise they are easy to grow. Spacing is important - if you space them widely you will get large onions but obviously there will be fewer of them. For medium sized onions space them 5cm, 2in apart in rows about 25cm, 10in apart. You could then thin them out slightly and use some as spring onions in May. Push the onion or shallot sets into the soil to half their depth. Look at them every couple of weeks and push any back in that have come right out of the ground. They do not like to be buried but prefer to grow on the surface. Onions and shallots require a little watering while the plants establish themselves but after that are best left unwatered. Shallots will be ready in July or August when the leaves have turned yellow. They will have formed clusters of small bulbs which have grown around the central set. You should lift them and leave them on the surface in the sun to dry. Then they can be divided and hung in a cool dry shed. In mid August the tops of your onions will bend over and this stops growth and exposes the bulbs to sunlight so that they can ripen. They will be ready for harvesting in September.

Shallots are milder than ordinary onions and work well in stews or you can pickle them. They can also be cut into rings for salads. Red onions are also milder and sweeter than white ones.

When you peel an onion the reaction of the enzymes in it being exposed to air causes your eyes to water. Try peeling your onions under running water as this can help. The juice of the onion is antiseptic and was said to cure baldness! The juice contains a substance that can delay blood clotting. Onions contain small amounts of vitamins and minerals but are thought to be beneficial because they contain flavonoids which may help fight against cancer, are a natural antibiotic and contain quercetin, an antioxidant.They are an essential ingredient of many recipes - here I have included recipes where the onion is the main ingredient.

Onions can of course be stored very successfully and stringing them up as a rope is the best way as it allows a flow of air to circulate around them.

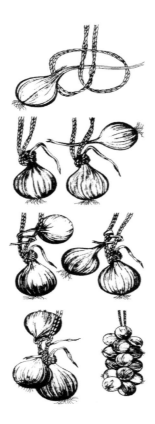

TOASTED CHEESE AND ONION SOUP
Serves 4

50g, 2oz butter
450g, 1lb onions, peeled and sliced into rings
1 tbsp flour
900ml, 1½pts vegetable stock

Topping
4 slices of French bread
50g, 2oz mature Cheddar cheese, sliced

Melt the butter in a large saucepan and fry the onions until well browned. Mix in the flour and then gradually add the stock. Simmer for 30 minutes. Toast the bread and divide the cheese between the slices. Grill until golden and bubbling. Divide the soup between 4 bowls and top each with the toasted cheese.

ONION TART
Serves 4 – 6

225g, 8oz shortcrust pastry
25g, 1oz butter
75g, 3oz unsmoked back bacon, chopped
450g, 1lb onions, peeled and chopped
½ tsp caraway seeds
2 eggs
150ml, ¼pt soured cream

Roll out the pastry and use to line a greased 20cm, 8in flan tin. Fry the bacon in the butter for several minutes and add the onions. Fry slowly for another 10 minutes. Add the caraway seeds. Beat the eggs and soured cream together. Scatter the bacon and onion mixture over the pastry base. Pour the eggs and cream over the top and bake in the oven at gas mark 5, 190°C (375°F) for 30 minutes.

CRISP ONION RINGS
Serves 3 – 4

These are very easy and simple to make.

1 large red and 1 white onion, peeled
1 egg white
1 tbsp plain flour
pinch of salt
1 clove of garlic, peeled and crushed
oil for frying

Cut the onions into rings. Mix the flour into the egg white. Add the salt and garlic. Stir the onions into the batter. Heat the oil in a deep fat fryer or large frying pan and fry in small batches until brown and crisp. Drain any excess oil from the rings by patting them with kitchen roll and keep warm while you fry the rest.

ONION BHAJIS
Serves 4

1 egg + 2tbsp water
1 tsp lemon juice
75g, 3oz plain flour
¼ tsp turmeric
¼ tsp ground cumin
¼ tsp ground coriander
1 red and 1 white onion, peeled and sliced
1 tbsp chives, chopped

Break the egg into a bowl and beat with the water and lemon juice. Beat in the flour with the spices. This will make a thick batter. Add the onions and chives and mix well to coat. Heat enough oil in a pan to deep fry the bhajis and drop spoonfuls of the mixture in. Fry in batches until golden which should only take 3 or 4 minutes. Drain on kitchen paper. Serve with mango chutney.

ONION AND APPLE CHUTNEY

Makes about 2kg, 4½lb

1kg, 2.2lb onions, peeled and chopped
1kg, 2.2lb apples, peeled and chopped
1 tsp dry mustard
1 tbsp ground ginger
450g, 1lb sultanas
1kg, 2.2lb tomatoes, skinned
175g, 6oz sugar
1 tbsp salt
1.2 litres, 2pts white wine vinegar

Mix all the ingredients together in a large pan and bring the mixture to the boil, then turn down and simmer over a low heat for 2 hours, stirring every so often. Pot and seal.

RED ONION MARMALADE
Makes about ½kg, 1lb

6 tbsp olive oil
1kg, 2.2lb red onions, peeled and sliced
6 tbsp demerara sugar
4 tbsp sherry vinegar

Heat the oil in a pan, add the onions and sugar. Cook for about 1½ hours on a low heat, stirring every so often to prevent the onions from sticking. Add the vinegar and cook for another 30 minutes.

PARSNIPS

Parsnips have been cultivated around the eastern Mediterranean since ancient times. Certainly the Greeks and Romans used parsnips – Pliny refers to pastinaca, probably meaning carrots and parsnips, in the first century AD. Parsnips were sent to Emperor Tiberius in Rome every year from Germany where they grew in profusion along the Rhine Valley. It is possible that the Celts of that part of Europe had brought the parsnip back from their travels to the East hundreds of years before. In the Middle Ages the roots were used for medicinal purposes such as treating toothache, swollen testicles and stomach aches. In the sixteenth century parsnips were a common vegetable, being one of the staples of the poorer people of Europe. English colonists must have introduced parsnips to America as there is evidence that they were being grown in Virginia in 1609. It is also known that parsnips were used as animal fodder in Europe in the sixteenth century and today Italians still feed parsnips to the pigs bred for best quality Parma ham.

The parsnip is a hardy biennial. It needs a deeply cultivated soil which has been manured for a previous crop. As with carrots, parsnips need stone free soil which is moisture retentive in order for the roots to develop fully. They take a long time to germinate (up to 1 month) therefore it is a good idea to sow them interspersed with radishes or with lettuces so that you do not lose track of where you have planted them. Seeds do not keep well so it is best to buy fresh seed every year. Even fresh seeds germinate irregularly so it is best to sow about 5 seeds in a cluster and then thin the seedlings that do develop. Traditionally parsnips are sown in February but in practice it is best to wait until March or April when the soil is warmer and you can even postpone until May and still get a good crop in late November. Seeds should be planted 1cm, ½in deep and depending on the variety of parsnips you use, should be in rows 30cm, 1ft apart for larger roots and 20cm, 8in apart for small types. Thin to 15cm, 6in apart for large varieties and 8cm, 3in apart for smaller varieties. The seeds are very thin like confetti, and consist of a very thin membranous disc which can, in cold soil, become covered with fungus and therefore fail to germinate. If you want to grow really large, prize-winning parsnips you can take a crow bar and make a 60cm, 2ft hole in the ground. Make a circular movement in the hole to create a funnel shape. Then fill the hole with John Innes compost and plant a few seeds in a circle at the top. Cover with a little compost. Thin to the strongest seedling once the seeds have germinated. Seeds sown in March will produce parsnips ready for harvesting in October/November so they will occupy your patch for a long time. You should not encounter too many problems once the roots start to develop and will only need to hoe and weed between the parsnips. In any case leave your parsnips in the soil until they have been exposed to a couple of frosts as this will improve their flavour.

Parsnip canker can develop when wet weather in the autumn follows a particularly dry spell – this causes the crown of the root to crack which may then be invaded by fungi causing the root to go black and rot.

Recommended varieties are Avonresister (which is resistant to Canker) Tender and True, Gladiator and White Gem.

Parsnips contain some Vitamin C, B1, and beta-carotene and are a reasonable source of iron. They also contain a natural sweetness so were used in cakes in Medieval times before sugar as we know it was developed (sugar beet was not developed until the nineteenth century) and indeed parsnips have a higher content of sugar than sugar beet. I have included a parsnip, date and ginger loaf which contains parsnip and honey to sweeten it (see page 128). Parsnips were also used to make wine and beer in the past. For cooking you will need to peel or scrub your parsnips and if the centre core is tough it is best removed. Sliced parsnips are delicious roasted in the oven round a joint or in a little oil.

CURRIED PARSNIP AND APPLE SOUP
Serves 4 – 6

25g, 1oz butter
1 tbsp oil
225g, 8oz onions, peeled and chopped
1 tbsp curry powder
450g, 1lb parsnips, sliced
225g, 8oz cooking apples, peeled and chopped
600ml, 1pt chicken stock
150ml, ¼pt milk
150ml, ¼pt white wine
salt and pepper
2 crisp eating apples, cored and chopped

Melt the butter and oil in a heavy saucepan and add the chopped onions. Then stir in the curry powder, parsnips and cooking apples. Cook together gently for 10 minutes. Add the stock, milk and wine, bring to the boil and simmer for 30 minutes or until the parsnips are soft. Purée in a food processor or blender. Reheat and if liked add the two chopped eating apples just before serving.

PARSNIP AND TOMATO SOUP
Serves 4 – 6

25g, 1oz butter
2 onions, peeled and chopped
1 clove of garlic, peeled and crushed
450g, 1lb parsnips, peeled and chopped
3 tbsp flour
salt and pepper
1 tsp thyme, chopped
900ml, 1½pts vegetable stock
150ml, ¼pt milk
350g, 12oz tomatoes, skinned and chopped

Melt the butter in a large saucepan and fry the onions for 5 minutes. Add the garlic and parsnips and fry for several more minutes. Stir in the flour, seasoning and thyme and then add the stock, milk and tomatoes. Cover and simmer for about 30 minutes. Purée in a blender or processor and then return to the pan and reheat gently. Serve immediately.

GLAZED PARSNIPS
Serves 6 as a side dish

4 parsnips, peeled
25g, 1oz butter
25g, 1oz brown sugar
squeeze of lemon juice
3 tbsp cider

Halve the parsnips and par-boil them for 5 minutes. Lay in a greased ovenproof dish and dot with butter. Sprinkle the brown sugar and a little lemon juice over them and pour the cider into the dish. Bake in the oven at gas mark 5, 190°C (375°F) for 30 minutes or until the parsnips are golden and glazed.

CHEESY PARSNIP AND TOMATO BAKE
Serves 4

450g, 1lb parsnips, peeled and sliced
300ml, ½pt single cream
1 tbsp brown sugar
75g, 3oz Cheddar cheese, grated
450g, 1lb tomatoes, sliced
3 tbsp brown breadcrumbs
25g, 1oz butter

Grease a small casserole dish and layer parsnips over the bottom of the dish. Sprinkle some of the cream, sugar and cheese over them and then top with a layer of tomatoes. Continue the layers in this way ending with the rest of the cream and cheese. Scatter the breadcrumbs over the top and dot with the butter. Bake in the oven at gas mark 5, 190°C (375°F) for about 30 minutes.

PARSNIP, CARROT AND APPLE ROAST
Serves 6

This goes well with a simple meat dish.

450g, 1lb carrots, peeled and chopped
900g, 2lb parsnips, peeled and chopped
6 tbsp olive oil
4 level tsp soft brown sugar
salt and pepper
4 Granny Smiths or other crisp eating apples, peeled, cored
and chopped

Mix the carrots and parsnips with the oil, sugar, salt and pepper. Place the chopped apples in a roasting tin and top with the vegetables. Bake in the oven for 1 hour at gas mark 6, 200°C (400°F).

PARSNIP CROQUETTES
Serves 4

450g, 1lb parsnips
75g, 3oz butter
1 egg, beaten
2 tbsp single cream
1 tsp lemon juice
2 tbsp flour + 1 beaten egg
50g, 2oz breadcrumbs
oil for frying

Cook the parsnips in salted water until tender. Mash them up with the butter and over a gentle heat add the egg, cream and lemon juice. Stir everything together until smooth. Allow to cool and then shape into sausage shapes. Coat with flour, then with egg and lastly with breadcrumbs. Fry in batches in oil in a large frying pan.

PARSNIP AND CARROT PURÉE
Serves 4 – 6

450g, 1lb parsnips, peeled and chopped
225g, 8oz carrots, scraped or peeled and chopped
25g, 1oz butter
1 tbsp double cream
salt and pepper

Cook the carrots and parsnips in salted water until just tender. Purée with the butter and cream and add salt and pepper to taste.

PARSNIP, DATE AND GINGER LOAF
Serves 6 – 8

350g, 12oz self-raising flour
½ tsp bicarbonate of soda
½ tsp nutmeg
½ tbsp ginger
225g, 8oz parsnips, peeled and grated
175g, 6oz margarine
125g, 5oz clear honey
100g, 4oz dates, chopped
1 egg
1 tbsp milk

Sift the flour, bicarbonate of soda and spices. Stir in the parsnips. Melt the margarine with the honey and add the dates. Stir this mixture into the dry ingredients and add the egg and milk. Mix everything together until well combined. Spoon into a greased 450g, 1lb loaf tin and bake in the oven at gas mark 4, 180°C (350°F) for about 30 minutes or until a skewer inserted comes out clean. Leave in the tin to cool for 10 minutes before turning out.

Young shallot plants (see page 116)

A young broad bean plant
(see page 20)

Purple sprouting broccoli which we enjoyed through March and April (see page 24)

Our hens enjoying a broccoli plant we had finished with.

A bowl of
Beetroot and
Tomato Soup
(see page 16)

Beetroot, Spinach and Mackerel Salad (see page 17)

Curly Kale (the variety is Pentland Brig) which we enjoyed through January to April (see page 100)

Carrot and Kale with Poppy Seeds (see page 49)

Stuffed Pepper Soufflés (see page 143)

French Beans sautéed with Red Pepper (see page 92)

Pea Tarts (see page 133)

Spinach
Soufflé
(see page
169)

Radicchio, Egg and Avocado Salad (see page 71)

Roasted Squash with Courgette and Tomato (see page 155)

Carrot and
Apple Tart
(see
page 49)

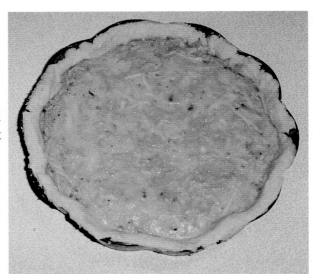

Wholemeal Pumpkin and Lemon Cake (see page 158)

PEAS AND MANGETOUT

I eat my peas with honey,
I've done it all my life.
It makes the peas taste funny
But it keeps 'em on my knife!
Anon

Peas are one of the oldest vegetables. Evidence of peas has been found in Burma and they were dated at 9750BC. By the Bronze Age they were being eaten by the peoples of Central Europe and seeds have been found in Switzerland. In these ancient times the peas were dried and formed an important part of the diet because they could be stored and provided protein during winter when other vegetables were scarce. We do not know whether peas arrived it Italy and Greece from Switzerland or from the East via India. The Romans and Greeks were cultivating peas around 500BC. The Romans probably introduced them to Britain. Their Latin name is Pisum Sativum and at first in Britain they were known as pease. It was not until the eighteenth century that they became 'peas'. Meanwhile in France Catherine de Medici married Henry II in 1533 and brought many of her favourite foods from her Italian homeland including piselli novelli. These new little peas were so much more tasty than dried peas and soon caught on, becoming known as petit pois, still used today. The French court was so keen on green peas that in Paris in 1696 Madame de Maintenoy wrote to Cardinal de Noailles – 'there are some ladies who, having supped, and supped well, take peas at home before going to bed… it's a fashion, a craze.'

Another type of pea, the edible podded pea, which is harvested when the peas are immature so that the whole pod is eaten is called mangetout from the French 'eat-all'. Mangetout is also known in other parts of the world as snow pea, Chinese pea or sugar pea. Then there are asparagus peas which are also known as winged peas – these do not have seeds and are eaten whole. They have a flavour similar to asparagus.

Peas can be sown any time from March through until early June. Sow 7.5cm, 3in apart. You could sow at two or three week intervals to give yourself peas over a longer period. Mangetout are particularly nice to grow as they expensive to buy – a good variety to try is Carouby de Maussane which grows like a runner bean plant but has purple flowers and flat thin pods; Sugar Dwarf Sweet Green and Oregon Sugar Pods are also popular. Sugar Snap peas are fun to grow and can be eaten raw in salads as well as lightly cooked. You should protect the growing plants against birds and keep them weed free. All but the dwarf varieties will need support. Do not water in the early stages of growth as this will result in too many leaves - water when the plants begin to flower and when the pods are forming water twice a week to increase the yield. Pick the pods when they are fat but still green and juicy. Both peas and mangetout become available fairly early on in the season, usually June and July. Half a kilo or a pound of peapods will produce about half that amount in peas. You can use the peapods to make a summer soup. See recipe on the opposite page.

Peas were the first ever vegetable to be canned or frozen. They are a very good source of Vitamin C, A and B and potassium.

PEAPOD SOUP
Serves 3 – 4

300ml, ½pt milk
300ml, ½pt vegetable stock
450g, 1lb peapods
1 bay leaf
4 mint leaves
salt and pepper
3 tbsp single cream

Put the pods, milk, stock and herbs in a saucepan, cover and simmer until the pods are tender which could take up to 1 hour depending on the size of pods. Discard the bay leaf and mint. Rub the peapod mixture through a sieve. Using a food processor is no good because you need to leave the stringy bits behind. Season it, reheat and add a little single cream to each portion if liked.

PEA, LEMON AND SORREL SOUP
Serves 8

1 tbsp olive oil
1 onion, peeled and chopped
bunch of sorrel, about 12 large leaves
1.5 litres, 2½pts chicken stock
450g, 1lb fresh or frozen peas
salt and pepper
grated rind of 1 lemon

Heat the oil in a large saucepan and cook the onion until soft. Throw in the sorrel leaves and stir until wilted. Pour in the stock and bring to the boil. Add the peas, salt and pepper and simmer for 15 minutes. Purée and sieve the soup. Return to a clean saucepan, heat through and add the grated lemon rind.

PEA, PEAR AND MINT SOUP
Serves 8

This soup can be served hot or cold. If you decide to serve it cold, swirl a dollop of crème fraîche into each bowl of soup before serving.

3 tbsp sunflower oil
2 onions, skinned and chopped
450g, 1lb peas, fresh or defrosted if frozen
3 pears, peeled, cored and chopped
1.2 litres, 2pts chicken stock
salt and pepper
juice of ½ a lemon
a handful of apple mint (just the leaves)

Cook the chopped onions in the oil in a saucepan for 5 minutes. Then add the peas, chopped pears and the chicken stock. Half-cover the pan with a lid and simmer for 20 minutes. Process or liquidize the soup and season with salt, pepper and lemon juice. Lastly, chop the mint leaves and stir them into the soup.

FRENCH STYLE CREAMY PEAS AND LETTUCE
Serves 4

25g, 1oz butter
6 spring onions, chopped
1 iceberg lettuce
450g, 1lb peas
pinch of sugar
Salt and pepper
60ml, 2fl oz vegetable stock
2 tbsp cream (optional)

Melt the butter in a small casserole and add the spring onions. Cut the iceberg lettuce into quarters and lay on top of the onions. Add the peas, pinch of sugar and seasoning and pour the stock over the vegetables. Cover with a lid and cook gently for about 10 minutes. The liquid should have been absorbed. Stir in the cream if using and serve.

PEA TARTS
Makes 8 small tarts - see photo in colour section

Spiced cheese pastry (see page 106)
125g, 5oz peas, lightly cooked
pinch of sugar
1 tbsp cream cheese
a couple of mint leaves
diced red pepper for garnish

Roll out the cheese pastry and use to line 8 greased tartlet tins. Bake blind until golden brown. Purée the peas with the sugar, cream cheese and mint. Fill the tarts with the pea purée and decorate with small pieces of red pepper.

RISI E BISI – RICE WITH PEAS
Serves 4 – 6

This is a famous dish from Venice – it is a cross between a soup and a risotto dish.

2 tbsp olive oil
50g, 2oz butter
4 rashers unsmoked bacon, diced
1 onion, peeled and chopped
225g, 8oz arborio rice
1 tsp sugar
1.5 litres, 2½pts chicken stock
225g, 8oz peas, either fresh or frozen
50g, 2oz Parmesan cheese, grated
salt and pepper

Heat the oil and butter in a large frying pan and fry the bacon and onion. Add the rice and sugar and stir around to coat in the buttery juices. Add half the stock and simmer uncovered, stirring frequently until the rice is absorbed. Add the rest of the stock along with the peas and simmer until almost all the stock has been absorbed. If you are using frozen peas, defrost them and throw them in when the rice is almost cooked for the last 5 minutes of cooking time. Now take the pan off the heat and stir in the remaining butter, half the cheese and season with salt and pepper. Allow to rest for a couple of minutes and then serve sprinkled with the rest of the Parmesan.

PEA PURÉE WITH NOODLES AND BACON
Serves 4

175g, 6oz peas or 450g, 1lb peas in their pods
100g, 4oz onion, peeled and chopped
100g, 4oz unsmoked bacon
120ml, 4fl oz vegetable stock
½ tsp sugar
225g, 8oz noodles
150ml, ¼pt soured cream

Add the peas, onion, and sugar to the stock and bring to the boil. Boil for 5 minutes and liquidize to make a purée. Meanwhile fry the bacon in its own fat and chop it up. Cook the noodles. Reheat the purée and stir in the soured cream. Pour the pea purée over the noodles and sprinkle the bacon on top.

PEA AND BEEF MEATBALLS
Serves 3 – 4

100g, 4oz peas
1 onion, peeled and grated
225g, 8oz minced beef
50g, 2oz brown breadcrumbs
1 tsp mint, chopped
1 egg
flour for coating
olive oil for frying

Bring some water to the boil and cook the peas. Purée them and mix in the onion, minced beef, breadcrumbs, mint and egg. Shape into patties, coat in flour and fry in the olive oil in a large frying pan on both sides until browned and cooked. Serve with tomato sauce and pasta or rice.

MANGETOUT AND APPLE SALAD
WITH TOASTED HAZELNUTS
Serves 4

This makes a healthy refreshing salad.

350g, 12oz mangetout, topped and tailed
2 Cox's apples, cored and chopped
50g, 2oz toasted hazelnuts

Dressing

4 tbsp olive oil
2 tbsp hazelnut or walnut oil
2 tbsp cider vinegar
salt and pepper
1 tsp grain mustard

Blanch the mangetout in boiling water for a couple of minutes. Drain and run cold water over them to keep them green. Put in a serving bowl with the chopped apples. Make the dressing by combining the oils, vinegar, mustard and seasoning. Pour over the apple and mangetout. Chop the hazelnuts and scatter over the salad. Serve at once.

MANGETOUT AND BACON SALAD
Serves 4 – 6

450g, 1lb mangetout or sugar snap peas
100g, 4oz unsmoked bacon, chopped
100g, 4oz Feta cheese, crumbled
50g, 2oz croutons

Dressing
4 tbsp olive oil
½ tbsp lemon juice
½ tbsp white wine vinegar

Trim the ends of the mangetout and blanch in boiling salted water for a couple of minutes. Arrange in a serving bowl. Dry fry the bacon and scatter over the mangetout along with the crumbled Feta cheese and the croutons. Make the dressing by combining all the ingredients and shaking them together in a screw topped jar. Pour over the salad and serve.

PASTA WITH TUNA AND MANGETOUT
Serves 3 – 4

450g, 1lb penne or fusilli
175g, 6oz mangetout or sugar snap peas, topped and tailed
25g, 1oz butter
150ml, ¼pt soured cream
185g, 7oz tin of tuna in oil
75g, 3oz Parmesan cheese, grated

Cook the pasta according to the packet's instructions. Steam the mangetout for 2 or 3 minutes. When the pasta is cooked, drain and return to the saucepan. Over a very low heat stir in the butter, soured cream and tuna with some of the oil from the tin. Add the mangetout. Serve immediately sprinkled with the Parmesan.

TURKEY AND MANGETOUT STIR FRY
Serves 3 – 4

A nutritious meal which is reasonably low in calories and quick to prepare.

2 tbsp olive oil
450g, 1lb turkey breast cut into strips
100g, 4oz carrots, peeled and sliced into strips
225g, 8oz mangetout, topped and tailed
225g, 8oz bean sprouts
2 tbsp soya sauce
350g, 12oz noodles

Heat the oil in a wok and stir fry the turkey strips for a couple of minutes. Add the carrots and after a couple more minutes the mangetout. Stir fry for a few minutes and then add the bean sprouts and soya sauce. Heat through. Cook the noodles according to the packet instructions and serve the turkey and mangetout over portions of noodles. Add more soya sauce if liked.

PEPPERS

There are two types of pepper: sweet peppers and hot chilli peppers - both are fruits of the Capsicum plant and originated in Central and South America. Seeds have been found in Mexican settlements and dated at around 7000BC and the Aztecs are known to have grown them. Columbus discovered them in the New World and Spanish and Portuguese explorers then distributed them around the world. Peppers were being used in Britain by the mid 1500s. Nowadays Spain and Hungary make an industry of producing peppers and paprika (the dried and ground powder of peppers). Chilli peppers are used to make cayenne pepper. I am only dealing with sweet peppers here.

Green, yellow and red peppers have only become popular in Britain relatively recently. Peppers are best grown in pots and can mature outside in the southern milder parts of Britain, preferably in a sheltered sunny spot against a south wall. Otherwise they need to be grown in greenhouses or under cloches. Seeds can be sown in pots in early March but the temperature needs to be around 60°F, 16°C. You could then transplant them to bigger pots and leave them outside from June onwards. Alternatively you can buy seedlings from a Garden Centre and pot them on. Once the flowers appear, nip out the first ones to encourage fruiting. Pick out the ends of the side shoots once about four fruit have set. This will concentrate the plant into producing a few good peppers. You may need to support the plants with small stakes. Feed once a week with liquid fertiliser. The peppers will become green and can be picked at this stage but are not so sweet. If left, they will turn orange and then red in the sun. There are some unusual brown or black varieties available if you want to be really exotic.

Peppers are richer in Vitamin C than any other vegetable and red peppers are very high in beta-carotene. They will keep for up to two weeks in the fridge without losing their nutrients.

STUFFED PEPPERS
Serves 4

Serve with a tomato sauce.

4 green peppers
1 tbsp olive oil
1 clove of garlic, crushed
1 onion, peeled and chopped
225g, 8oz minced beef
1 egg, beaten
1 tbsp breadcrumbs
salt and pepper
1 tbsp fresh parsley, chopped
1 tbsp fresh chives, chopped
water

Cut the stalk end of the peppers off and keep them. Remove the seeds and blanch the peppers in a pan of boiling salted water for a couple of minutes. Then turn upside down to drain. Heat the oil in a pan and fry the garlic and onion until softened. Add the minced beef and cook until browned. Stir together the egg and breadcrumbs and add to the meat with seasoning and the herbs. Spoon the stuffing into the peppers and put the lids on. Arrange close together in an ovenproof dish and pour over a little water. Bake in the oven at gas mark 5, 190°C (375°F) for 30 minutes.

CANNELLONI STUFFED WITH TUNA AND RED PEPPERS
Serves 4

50g, 2oz butter
100g, 4oz mushrooms, chopped
1 large red pepper, deseeded and chopped
1 clove of garlic, peeled and crushed
1 x 185g, 7oz tin of tuna, drained
50g, 2oz brown breadcrumbs
12 oven-ready cannelloni

For the sauce

25g, 1oz butter
25g, 1oz flour
300ml, ½pt milk
75g, 3oz mature Cheddar cheese, grated
50g, 2oz Parmesan, grated

Melt the butter in a frying pan and sauté the mushrooms and chopped pepper for 2 or 3 minutes. Add the garlic, tuna and breadcrumbs and cook for about 5 minutes. To make the sauce melt the butter, stir in the flour and gradually add the milk. Stir in the Cheddar cheese. Stuff the cannelloni with the tuna mixture. Pour a little of the cheese sauce into the bottom of an ovenproof dish and arrange the cannelloni on top. Pour over the rest of the sauce so that the cannelloni are covered and sprinkle with the Parmesan cheese. Bake in the oven at gas mark 5, 190°C (375°F) for 30 minutes until golden brown.

RED PEPPER, SPINACH AND TOMATO RISOTTO
Serves 4

25g, 1oz butter
1 onion, peeled and chopped
2 red peppers
10 sun-dried tomatoes, sliced
350g, 12oz arborio rice
150ml, ¼pt white wine
1 litre, 1¾pts vegetable stock
1 handful of spinach, shredded
50g, 2oz Parmesan cheese, grated

Heat the butter in a large frying pan and cook the onion until soft. Add the peppers, sun-dried tomatoes and rice. Stir to coat in the juices and then gradually add the wine and stock, stirring all the time as the liquid gets absorbed. When the rice is tender and all the liquid has been absorbed, stir in the spinach and cheese. Cook for a couple of minutes and serve straightaway.

SWEET PEPPER AND HERB FLAN
Serves 4 – 6

225g, 8oz shortcrust pastry
3 peppers, 1 green, 1 yellow and 1 red
175g, 6oz Boursin cheese
2 eggs
handful of rocket
1 tbsp fresh parsley, chopped

Roll out the pastry and use to line a greased 20cm, 8in flan tin. Bake blind in the oven at gas mark 4, 180°C (350°F) for 15 minutes. Grill the peppers until their skins are charred. Cool and peel off the black skin. Cut the peppers up into small pieces. Whisk together the Boursin cheese and eggs and mix in the rocket, parsley and peppers. Spoon this mixture into the flan case and bake at gas mark 4, 180°C (350°F) for another 25 minutes.

PIPERADE
Serves 2

A dish of eggs and vegetables, traditionally peppers and tomatoes.

50g, 2oz butter
1 onion, peeled and chopped
2 cloves of garlic, peeled and chopped
2 red peppers, deseeded and sliced
3 tomatoes, chopped
4 eggs
1 tbsp fresh parsley, chopped

Melt the butter in a pan and add the onion and garlic. Then add the peppers and tomatoes and sauté gently until soft. Whisk the eggs and add to the vegetables with the parsley. Cook for 4 or 5 minutes. Serve perhaps on toast or accompanied by hot rolls.

STUFFED PEPPER SOUFFLÉS
Serves 4 - great as a starter for a supper party - see photo in colour section

4 peppers, all red or a mixture of red and green
25g, 1oz butter
25g, 1oz flour
240ml, 8fl oz milk
50g, 2oz extra mature Cheddar cheese, grated
2 eggs, separated

Cut the stalk end of the peppers and discard. Remove the seeds and blanch the peppers in a pan of boiling water for a couple of minutes. Drain and turn upside down. Make the soufflé mixture by melting the butter in a saucepan, stirring in the flour and gradually adding the milk until you have a smooth sauce. Stir in the egg yolks and the cheese. Whisk the egg whites and fold them in. Arrange the peppers in a baking tin and fill with the soufflé mixture. Cook in the oven at gas mark 4, 180°C (350°F) for 20 minutes.

POTATOES

Potatoes originated in the subtropical regions of the Andes in Peru and Chile. Spanish Conquistadors conquered Peru in 1536, discovered the potato and brought it back to Spain. Sir John Hawkins is thought to have brought potatoes to Britain in 1563. Sir Francis Drake had potatoes brought to his ship when, during his circumnavigation of the world in 1580, he was anchored off the coast of Peru. The local Indians apparently brought him potatoes and a pig as a gift. Drake then brought these back to Britain. Sir Walter Raleigh about the same time brought potatoes back and planted them at his home in County Cork in Ireland; he also presented them to Elizabeth I. From Spain the potato gradually spread through other parts of Europe. At first these potatoes were regarded with suspicion. The potato comes from the same family as the deadly nightshade and potato leaves and flowers are poisonous. In France and Germany they were thought to cause leprosy but gradually people began to recognize the potato as a medicinal plant and herbalists claimed that it could cure all sorts of illnesses ranging from diarrhoea to TB. Later on they were thought to be an aphrodisiac. In the 1740s Frederick the Great, King of Prussia and King William of Germany began campaigns to introduce potatoes to their empires. Indeed Frederick the Great had to enforce his orders by threatening to cut off the nose and ears of anybody who refused to plant and eat potatoes. At this time the French pharmacist Parmentier, who was imprisoned by the Prussians during the Seven Years War (1756 – 1763) discovered the benefits of the potato which he claimed were responsible for his survival. He subsequently studied the potato and looked for ways to improve its quality. His views clashed with those of the peasants who saw the potato as a food suitable only for pigs. He overcame this by planting potatoes over a 50 acre plot and employing guards, by day only, to protect the crop. During the night the peasants, thinking this a valuable crop indeed, slipped over the wall and stole the potatoes to grow themselves. A bit of greedy curiosity led to potatoes becoming all the rage. Parmentier helped King Louis XVI popularise them by creating a feast with only potato dishes: he developed potato soup still known today as Potage Parmentier, Omelette Parmentier and created 'French fries'. He presented Louis XVI with a bouquet of potato flowers and Marie Antoinette wore them in her hair. The King also gave the potato its French name pomme de terre (earth apple). Before that time it had been known as batata.

By the early 1800s the potato had become firmly established. Scotland and Ireland were particularly keen on growing them but in 1845 the failure of the crop in Ireland through blight caused devastating famine. The North Americans probably first experienced the potato through Irish immigrants in the eighteenth century.

There are many different varieties of potatoes including early ones to use as new potatoes and maincrop potatoes which are harvested in August. You should obtain seed potatoes in February and chit them. This involves placing them in single layers on trays or in egg boxes in a shed. You should place them rose end up (that is the end with the most eyes from which sprouts are starting to form). The temperature should be between 4°C and 10°C. You should leave the potatoes for about six to eight weeks and they do need light (but not direct sunlight) – leaving them in total darkness would result in them producing long but weak shoots. You should plant your tubers in March or early April. You need to dig holes and allow 5cm, 2in of soil to cover them. You should plant them with shoots uppermost and they should be 23cm, 9in apart in rows 60cm, 2ft apart. You should then earth up the potato plants once established in May. This means you create a mound of earth round the plants as this helps protect them from frost and prevents the developing potatoes near the surface from turning green as it excludes the light. There is usually enough moisture in the soil in April and May so you don't need to water at this stage. During dry weather you should water on a weekly basis as potatoes hate water accumulating around their roots. Early potatoes are usually ready for lifting when the plants are in full flower in June/July. Use a fork as a lever to lift the plant and collect the potatoes that have formed at the end of the roots. Maincrop potatoes should be planted in the same way with a little more room between the rows and these are not lifted until the tops have died down, usually in September.

Potatoes mainly consist of complex carbohydrates in the form of starch but also contain water and protein and are high in Vitamin C and potassium. The skins are an excellent source of fibre. New potatoes should be cooked and eaten as soon after lifting as possible as the sugars begin to convert to starch straightaway. A potato left too long in the light will begin to turn green and this green skin contains a substance called solanine which can cause illness if eaten.

I am not going to include straightforward recipes for roasting, frying, and mashing potatoes but here some more unusual things to do with your potatoes.

CRISPY POTATO SKINS
Serves 4 – 6

4 large baking potatoes
approx 3 tbsp olive oil
2 tsp paprika
sprinkling of Maldon sea salt

Prick the potatoes with a fork and bake in the oven at gas mark 5, 190°C (375°F) for 45 minutes so that they are partially cooked. Now slit each one in half and then into quarters. Scoop out some of the flesh from each one so that you are left with 16 boat shapes. Place on a greased baking tray and pour a little olive oil over each one and sprinkle paprika and salt over them. Bake in the oven for a further 30 minutes or until the skins look golden and crisp. Serve at once either with your main course or with a dip at a drinks party.

POTATO PANCAKES
Serves 4

450g, 1lb old potatoes, peeled
1 onion, peeled
1 tbsp flour
1 clove of garlic, peeled and crushed
1 egg, beaten
olive oil for frying

Grate the potatoes and onion and mix together with the flour. Add the garlic and egg. The mixture will have the consistency of thick cream. Drop spoonfuls of it into a frying pan of hot oil. Press the fritters down with a fish slice and fry on both sides. They should be crisp on the outside and soft in the middle.

BAKED LAYERED POTATOES
Serves 4 – 6

This is a cross between the French potatoes Lyonnaise and Dauphinois. The traditional Lyonnaise dish is sliced potato baked with onion and the usual Dauphinois consists of layers baked in cream and cheese. My version combines onion and milk.

1kg, 2.2lb potatoes, peeled and par-boiled
1 onion, sliced finely into rings
150ml, ¼pt milk
25g, 1oz butter
salt and pepper

Slice the par-boiled potatoes and lay some of them over the bottom of a greased ovenproof dish. Scatter onion rings over them and continue with layers of potato and onion. Pour the milk over the top and dot with the butter cut into little pieces. Season with salt and pepper and cook in the oven at gas mark 4, 180°C (350°F) for 30 minutes or until golden and crisp around the edges.

CHEESY DUCHESS POTATOES
Serves 6 – 8

50g, 2oz butter
1kg, 2.2lb potatoes, peeled, cooked and puréed
2 egg yolks
50g, 2oz mature Cheddar cheese, grated
salt and pepper

Mix the butter into the puréed potato and over a low heat add the egg yolks, cheese and some salt and pepper. Beat until smooth. Place the mixture in a piping bag and pipe out pyramid shapes on to a greased baking sheet. Bake in a preheated oven at gas mark 5, 190°C (375°F) for 10 minutes.

BACON POTATO CAKES
Serves 4 – 6

675g, 1½lb potatoes, peeled and boiled
2 egg yolks
1 onion, peeled and chopped
3 tbsp olive oil
3 rashers unsmoked streaky bacon, chopped
1 tbsp fresh chives, chopped

Mash the cooked potato and leave to cool before beating in the egg yolks. Meanwhile fry the onion in a tablespoon of the olive oil and after a couple of minutes add the bacon. Cook until crisp. Mix the onion and bacon into the potato and stir in the chives. Shape into about 12 round potato cakes. Heat the rest of the oil in a large frying pan and cook the potato cakes in batches until browned on both sides.

POTATOES IN SPICY TOMATO SAUCE
Serves 4 – 6

450g, 1lb new potatoes, scrubbed
2 tbsp olive oil
2 garlic cloves, peeled and chopped
1 green chilli, deseeded and chopped
1 tsp paprika
400g, 14oz tin of tomatoes

Cook the potatoes until just tender. Heat the oil in a frying pan, add the garlic, chilli and paprika and fry for two minutes. Add the tomatoes and simmer for about 10 minutes until the sauce is reduced and thick. Cut the potatoes into chunks and add to the tomato sauce. Stir around so that the potatoes are covered with sauce and serve warm or cold.

BACON, EGG AND POTATO BAKE
Serves 4

450g, 1lb potatoes, peeled and par-boiled
1 tbsp olive oil
100g, 4oz unsmoked bacon, chopped
1 onion, peeled and sliced
2 eggs
150ml, ¼pt milk
100g, 4oz mature Cheddar cheese, grated
1 tsp mixed herbs

Slice the par-boiled potatoes and lay half of them in a greased ovenproof dish. Fry the bacon with the onion in the olive oil and scatter over the potatoes. Cover with the rest of the potatoes. Beat together the eggs and milk and pour over the potato mixture. Sprinkle the grated cheese over the top along with the herbs. Bake in the oven for 40 minutes at gas mark 5, 190°C (375°F).

HOT POTATO SALAD
Serves 3 – 4

450g, 1lb new potatoes, scrubbed
2 hard-boiled eggs, chopped
2 tbsp olive oil
squeeze of lemon juice
2 tbsp mayonnaise
1 tbsp fresh chives, chopped
1 tbsp fresh parsley, chopped

Cook the potatoes until just tender and drain them. Transfer to a serving dish and while still hot mix in the chopped eggs, olive oil, mayonnaise and lemon juice. Lastly scatter with the parsley and chives. Serve at once.

POTATO DROP SCONES
Makes about 12

450g, 1lb floury potatoes, such as Maris Piper
25g, 1oz butter
100g, 4oz plain flour

Cook the potatoes until tender, then drain and mash them. Add the butter and work in the flour until you have a stiff dough. On a floured surface knead the mixture until smooth and then roll out and cut into rounds. Fry in a heavy based pan or greased griddle for a few minutes on each side and serve hot with butter and jam.

DATE AND CHOCOLATE SPREAD
Makes about 450g, 1lb but only keeps for a few days

100g, 4oz dates
25g, 1oz cocoa powder
75g, 3oz potatoes, mashed

Put the dates with 150ml, 5fl oz water and the cocoa powder in a small saucepan and heat gently to soften the dates. Transfer to a food processor and whiz until smooth. Mix in the mashed potato. If you are on a no sugar diet this is a useful sweet spread to eat on toast. Alternatively you could use it to fill a cake.

POTATO BISCUITS
Makes about 24

100g, 4oz margarine
225g, 8oz wholemeal flour
25g, 1oz caster sugar
75g, 3oz potatoes, peeled, cooked and sieved

Rub the margarine into the flour. Stir in the sugar. Add the potato and knead until you have a smooth dough. You will find that there is enough moisture in the potato for everything to bind together. Roll out the dough onto a floured surface and cut out 5cm, 2in rounds. Bake on greased baking sheets for about 15 minutes in the oven at gas mark 5, 190°C (375°F).

POTATO BREAD
Serves 4

100g, 4oz mashed potato, sieved
350g, 12oz flour
1 tsp fresh thyme, chopped
1 tsp fresh parsley, chopped
2 tsp cream of tartar
1 tsp bicarbonate of soda
½ tsp salt
150ml, ¼pt milk

Mix all the ingredients together. Bind together with the milk and knead a little. Transfer to a greased 450g, 1lb loaf tin and cook in the oven at gas mark 4, 180°C (350°F) for 30 minutes.

CHOCOLATE CAKE
Serves 6 – 8

This is a delicious chocolate cake with a good texture.

175g, 6oz margarine
175g, 6oz caster sugar
100g, 4oz potatoes, peeled, cooked and sieved or well mashed
3 eggs
50g, 2oz dark chocolate
3 tbsp milk
175g, 6oz self-raising flour
1 tsp baking powder
40g, 1½oz cocoa powder

Filling

50g, 2oz butter
100g, 4oz icing sugar
1 tsp cocoa powder

Cream the margarine and sugar together. Beat in the potato and the eggs one at a time. Sieve the flour with the baking powder and cocoa and stir into the mixture. Melt the chocolate and milk together and add to the mixture. Stir until everything is well incorporated. Divide the mixture between 2 greased 20cm, 8in cake tins and level the top. Bake in the oven at gas mark 4, 180°C (350°F) for 25 minutes. Take out, allow to cool a little and turn out the cakes. For the filling cream together the butter, icing sugar and cocoa powder and sandwich the two cakes together.

PUMPKINS AND SQUASHES

Pumpkins and squashes originated in America and in particular in Mexico where it is thought they have been grown since 7000BC. The word pumpkin comes from the Greek word for melon – 'Pepon' – or cooked in the sun. The earlier word we used in English was 'pompion'. Squash on the other hand is an abbreviation from the North American word 'askutasquash' meaning eaten uncooked. Wild forms were originally gathered for their seeds. Varieties of squash and pumpkins arrived in Europe after the discovery of the New World in the 1500s.

There are many varieties of both trailing and bush types. There are summer squashes which include pattypans and crooknecks as well as courgettes (these are dealt with separately on page 72). Then there are autumn squashes such as vegetable spaghetti (its flesh comes away in strands and resembles spaghetti) and marrows (included with courgettes) and winter squashes which include all varieties of pumpkins - these come in all sorts of colours and shapes but they all taste virtually the same. Last year I grew winter squashes called Buttercup (pictured on back cover) which were very successful. The plants trailed all over the place and I had to keep cutting them back so that each plant only produced three or four fruits. However not all the squashes turned out the same size. I also tried Butternut Squash but was not so successful with these. Other varieties I am trying are Golden Delicious (red/orange heart shaped fruit with a sweet and nutty flavour), Delicata (which has small long fruit with white and green stripes) and Uchiki Kuri (a Japanese variety with orange pear-shaped fruit).

They are easy to grow but require lots of manure. It is best to grow the seeds in pots in a propagator or on a warm windowsill for transplanting when the danger of frosts has passed in late May/early June. They can be trailed over a trellis or you can make the trailing stems grow round a circle of pegs. To make sure you get decent sized squashes only allow two or three per plant and you can put an old tile or piece of wood under each squash or pumpkin as they develop to stop them rotting on damp soil. Alternatively grow your squashes through black plastic as this will also stop the fruits rotting. They do require lots of water. Once picked you can store your squashes and pumpkins for months in a cool, dry place.

Nutritionally pumpkins and squashes are high in beta-carotene and also contain vitamin C and folic acid. Orange fleshed varieties contain the carotenoid, phytoene which may help prevent some cancers. The pumpkin or squash seeds are edible (once roasted) and are a good source of B vitamins, phosphorus, iron and zinc. There is also an oil you can now buy made from pumpkin seeds.

Pumpkins and squashes are very versatile and can be used in soups and breads, roasted, puréed, baked in their skins or used in sweet dishes such as the traditional American pumpkin pie.

PUMPKIN AND TOMATO SOUP
Serves 4 – 6

2 tbsp olive oil
1 onion, peeled and chopped
450g, 1lb pumpkin flesh, chopped
100g, 4oz red lentils
1 clove of garlic, peeled and crushed
1 x 400g, 14oz tin of chopped tomatoes
1.2 litres, 2pts vegetable stock
juice of ½ a lemon
salt and pepper
150ml, ¼pt milk or single cream
1 tbsp fresh parsley, chopped

Heat the oil in a large saucepan and fry the onion until soft. Add the pumpkin, lentils, garlic, tomatoes and stock and bring to the boil. Simmer for 30 minutes, allow to cool and then purée. Add the lemon juice and stir in the milk or cream, reheating gently. Sprinkle with parsley and serve.

PUMPKIN AND LEMON SOUP
Serves 6

1 onion, peeled and sliced
50g, 2oz butter
450g, 1lb pumpkin, peeled and cut into chunks
225g, 8oz potatoes, peeled and sliced
1 garlic clove, peeled and crushed
1 tsp fresh thyme, chopped
1.2 litres, 2pts chicken stock
4 tbsp lemon juice
150ml, ¼pt double cream

Fry the onion in the butter in a large saucepan. Add the pumpkin, potatoes, garlic and thyme. Cover and cook slowly for 20 minutes. Add the stock with salt and pepper. Bring to the boil, lower the heat and simmer for 10 minutes. Purée the soup, flavour with the lemon juice and stir in the cream. Serve immediately.

ROASTED SQUASH WITH
COURGETTE AND TOMATO
Serves 3 – 4   - see photo in colour section

½ a butternut squash, peeled and cut into chunks
1 red onion, peeled and cut into quarters
2 courgettes, sliced
225g, 8oz tomatoes, quartered
3 tbsp extra virgin olive oil
salt and pepper
1 tbsp of chopped parsley, breadcrumbs and grated cheese

Put all the vegetables into an ovenproof dish and add the olive oil. Stir to coat the vegetables in the oil. Season and roast in the oven at gas mark 5, 190°C (375°F) for 30 minutes or until all the vegetables are soft. Sprinkle with parsley, breadcrumbs and cheese and finish under the grill. Serve as a side dish or with eggs for a quick supper.

SQUASH AND PEA FRITTERS
Serves 4 – 6

225g, 8oz peas
2 eggs, beaten
3 tbsp plain flour
25g, 1oz mature Cheddar cheese, grated
sprig of fresh thyme + 1 tsp fresh coriander, chopped
salt and pepper
½ a butternut squash, peeled and grated
2 tbsp olive oil + 1 tbsp lemon juice

Cook the peas in boiling, salted water and then purée them in a processor. Beat the eggs and beat in the flour, cheese, thyme and seasoning. Add the puréed peas and stir in the grated squash. Heat the oil in a frying pan and add tablespoons of the vegetable mixture. Fry on both sides until golden and serve sprinkled with lemon juice.

BUTTERNUT SQUASH RISOTTO WITH ROCKET
Serves 4 – 6

25g, 1oz butter
1 onion, peeled and chopped
2 garlic cloves, peeled and chopped
1 medium butternut squash, peeled and cut into cubes
350g, 12oz arborio rice
1.2 litres, 2pts vegetable stock
50g, 2oz Parmesan cheese, grated
handful of rocket

Melt the butter in a large frying pan and cook the onion and garlic until softened. Add the squash and then the rice and stir around to coat with the oil. Gradually add the stock spoon by spoon, letting it be absorbed before adding more. Add the rocket and cheese when all the liquid has been absorbed. Stir and serve.

SQUASH AND COURGETTE ROSTI
Serves 3 – 4

2 large courgettes
½ a butternut squash
butter and olive oil for frying

Grate the courgette and dab with kitchen towel to get rid of any moisture. Peel the squash and grate it. Mix the grated vegetables together. Heat the butter and oil together in a frying pan and fry the mixture, patting it down with a fish slice. Divide it into two, then turn them over and fry on the other side. Serve at once.

SAVOURY SQUASH BAKE
Serves 4

This has an interesting, delicate flavour and would go well with a meat dish or as part of a vegetarian meal.

2 eggs
1 tbsp milk
225g, 8oz butternut squash, peeled, cooked and puréed
25g, 1oz butter, melted
3 or 4 large chard or spinach leaves, shredded
25g, 1oz fresh brown breadcrumbs
½ an onion, peeled and grated
1 clove of garlic, peeled and crushed
1 tsp fresh parsley + ½ tsp fresh thyme, chopped
salt and pepper

Beat the eggs with the milk. Mix in the squash purée, butter, chard, breadcrumbs, onion and garlic. Stir in the herbs and season with salt and pepper. Transfer to an ovenproof dish and bake in the oven at gas mark 4, 180°C (350°F) for 30 minutes by which time the dish should be set.

WHOLEMEAL PUMPKIN AND LEMON CAKE
Serves 6 - see photo in colour section

This is similar to a carrot cake.

175g, 6oz wholemeal flour
2 tsp baking powder
1 tsp cinnamon
100g, 4oz grated pumpkin or squash
100g, 4oz margarine
100g, 4oz dark brown sugar
grated peel of 1 lemon
2 eggs
2 tbsp milk

Filling

50g, 2oz butter
100g, 4oz icing sugar
2 tsp lemon juice
grated peel of ½ a lemon

Put all the ingredients in a food processor and whiz until smooth or sift together the flour, baking powder and cinnamon. Add the grated pumpkin. Cream the margarine and brown sugar together. Beat the eggs and add to the margarine and sugar mixture, adding a little flour if the mixture begins to curdle. Gradually add all the flour and pumpkin along with the grated lemon peel and mix in the milk. Divide between 2 greased 15cm, 6in round cake tins and bake in the oven at gas mark 4, 180°C (350°F) for 25 minutes. Meanwhile make the filling by creaming together the butter and icing sugar and beating in the lemon juice and peel. Use this filling to sandwich the cakes together. Dust with icing sugar and serve.

PUMPKIN SCONES
Makes 8 scones

225g, 8oz pumpkin or squash cut into cubes
225g, 8oz self-raising flour
2 tsp baking powder
1 tsp ground ginger
50g, 2oz butter
50g, 2oz caster sugar
2 tsp milk

Cook the pumpkin cubes in boiling water for about 10 minutes. Drain and mash. Sift the flour, baking powder and ginger. Rub in the butter until the mixture resembles breadcrumbs. Stir in the sugar, the pumpkin purée and the milk to make a dough. Turn onto a floured surface and press down to a thickness of about 2.5cm, 1in. Cut out rounds and put them on a greased baking tray. Bake in the oven at gas mark 6, 200°C (400°F) for between 10 and 15 minutes. Serve warm with butter and jam if liked.

PUMPKIN AND PECAN MUFFINS
Makes 8 muffins

75g, 3oz margarine
100g, 4oz brown sugar
75g, 3oz black treacle
175g, 6oz cooked pumpkin or squash
1 egg
125g, 5oz plain flour
½ tsp bicarbonate of soda
½ tsp cinnamon + ½ tsp nutmeg
50g, 2oz pecans, chopped

Cream together the margarine and sugar. Stir in the black treacle, pumpkin and the egg. Sift together the flour, bicarbonate of soda and spices and beat into the muffin mixture. Fold in the pecans and spoon into muffin tins. Cook in the oven at gas mark 4, 180°C (350°F) for 20 minutes.

159

PUMPKIN PIE
Serves 6 – 8

Pumpkin pie is the traditional American Thanksgiving pie and there are many different versions. My version, despite the spices, proved popular with the children.

225g, 8oz shortcrust pastry
175g, 6oz pumpkin purée
75g, 3oz granulated sugar
75g, 3oz molasses
1 small tin of evaporated milk
2 eggs
½ tsp cinnamon
½ tsp ginger
pinch of nutmeg

Roll out the pastry and use to line a greased 20cm, 8in flan dish. Bake blind for 10 minutes in the oven at gas mark 4, 180°C (350°F). Mix together the purée, sugar, molasses, evaporated milk, eggs and spices. Pour into the pastry case and return to the oven for 20 minutes. Serve with cream or Greek yoghurt.

RADISHES

Radishes are one of the oldest vegetables and thought to be native to China. They spread to the Mediterranean and were much used by the Romans, Greeks and Egyptians. The Roman writer Pliny describes the radish as 'having a remarkable power of causing flatulence and belching and consequently a vulgar part of the diet.' Horace said that 'lettuces and radish excite the languid stomach'. The Greeks offered a radish modelled in gold to Apollo in the temple at Delphi, though only a beetroot in silver and a turnip of lead. Herodotus stated that the slaves working on the building of the pyramids were given radishes, onions and garlic as their rations.

They are one of the easiest vegetables to grow but are not particularly versatile. As soon as possible in the early spring you can plant radish seeds 1cm, ½in deep thinly in drills and thin them out after they have established themselves to about 2.5cm, 1in apart. Radishes grow quickly so they make a useful vegetable to grow in between parsnip and carrot seeds which take a long time to germinate. In this way you will know where you have planted your parsnips and carrots and you can pick the radishes well before the other vegetables have developed fully. Beware of sowing seeds too late in the season as the radishes will bolt in hot weather. Do not over water them as this will produce good leaves and poor roots. In dry weather water once a week.

Radishes contain vitamins B and C. The bite or tanginess that you can taste in a radish is due to the presence of mustard oil. Radishes are predominantly red but you can also get white, black, purple, yellow and green skinned types. The most popular traditional varieties are red such as Cherry Belle and Scarlet Globe. There are winter varieties that you can also grow. Recommended varieties are Round Black and Long Black Spanish – these are black, large and turnip sized. There is also China Rose which is large with pink skin but white flesh.

For fun you may want to make radish flowers – to do this cut off the root but leave a little bit of the green tip. Make about six to eight cuts from the stalk end in the radish and then leave in iced water for at least an hour – the radish will have curled out where you made the slits, like a flower.

RADISH SOUP
Serves 4 – 6

2 tbsp olive oil
1 onion, peeled and sliced
8 large cabbage leaves, sliced
1 tsp curry powder
350g, 12oz radishes, topped and tailed
900ml, 1½pts vegetable stock
300ml, ½pt milk
salt and pepper
1 tbsp tarragon, dried or fresh

Fry the onion in the olive oil for a few minutes. Add the cabbage and cook for a couple of minutes. Stir in the curry powder and add the radishes and stock. Cover and bring to the boil, then simmer for 20 minutes. Purée in a blender or processor and then return to the saucepan and reheat as you stir in the milk. Serve sprinkled with tarragon.

SAUTÉED RADISHES AND MANGETOUT
Serves 4 as a side dish

100g, 4oz mangetout or sugar snap peas, topped and tailed
175g, 6oz radishes, sliced
3 spring onions, chopped
1 tbsp lemon juice

In a large frying pan melt the butter and olive oil. Sauté the mangetout for about 3 minutes, then add the radishes, spring

162

onions, mustard seeds and the lemon juice. Cook for several more minutes. Serve immediately.

RADISH, COTTAGE CHEESE AND CUCUMBER SALAD
Serves 2

A useful, low calorie salad.

225g, 8oz cottage cheese
bunch of red radishes
½ a cucumber
1 yellow pepper
2 spring onions

Spoon the cottage cheese into a bowl. Slice the radishes and cucumber and dice the yellow pepper. Mix into the cottage cheese. Slice the spring onions and sprinkle over the cottage cheese salad.

ROASTED RADISHES AND ROOT VEGETABLES
Serves 4

3 medium sweet potatoes, peeled and cut into chunks
4 medium parsnips, peeled and cut into chunks
2 medium red onions, peeled and quartered
350g, 12oz radishes, topped and tailed
1 whole head of garlic, cut in half lengthwise
3 tablespoons olive oil
1 tsp fresh thyme, chopped

Place all the vegetables in a roasting tin and drizzle the olive oil over them. Add the thyme and some black pepper and salt. Roast for about 40 minutes in the oven at gas mark 5, 190°C (375°F). Discard the garlic and serve as a side dish.

SPINACH AND CHARD

Spinach originated in Persia – the word comes from a Persian word, 'aspanakh'. It was first cultivated for its medicinal properties. The Arabs introduced it to Europe in the thirteenth century but it wasn't introduced to Britain until the 1500s. Spinach did not arrive in America until the nineteenth century when there is evidence that Thomas Jefferson was growing it in his garden.

Swiss chard is a leaf beet and related to beetroot but I have included it with spinach as it is cooked in the same way. Perpetual spinach is also a spinach beet but not a true spinach. Other relatives, with leaves not unlike spinach are Good King Henry, a wild version which is perennial, and a mountain spinach, Orache. There is also another type, New Zealand spinach, which is not a true spinach – it's a spreading, straggly plant but also a tender perennial.

True spinach can be divided into two types: summer spinach with round smooth seeds and prickly-seeded varieties which are sown in the autumn and withstand winter conditions. Types to be recommended for the summer are Lazio, Bloomsdale and America. Winter varieties are Giant Winter, Monnopa (this variety has a low oxalic acid content) and Medania - If you sow these in September you will be picking the spinach in April. Perpetual spinach can also be sown in September as it is very winter hardy.

Spinach is easy to grow. The soil should be water retentive, free draining and not too acidic. Soaking spinach seeds overnight before sowing them will speed up germination. They should be sown in rows 30cm, 1ft apart and then thinned to 15cm, 6in apart along the row.   Spinach sown in April should be ready for picking in June. Do not allow the plants to dry out - they must be watered regularly. Summer sown spinach can be a problem as it may run to seed before leaves have developed. Spinach definitely prefers cool conditions - you could plant some spinach between rows of peas or beans so that it gets some shade.

If you are going to grow spinach you should devote a decent amount of space to it – you need to harvest quite a lot of spinach as it cooks down to a much smaller amount. The advantage is that most varieties of spinach work as a cut-and-come-again crop and can be picked as baby leaves for salads. Dishes cooked with spinach are often described as Florentine (as in Florentine Eggs) because the people of Florence were particularly fond of spinach.

Spinach should be washed well and can then be cooked briefly in just the water clinging to the leaves. It is a very nutritious vegetable being high in Vitamin A, iron and calcium but also contains oxalic acid (this hinders the absorption of the calcium and iron). Its iron content was in fact over-estimated for many years. It also contains folate, a B vitamin that helps prevent heart disease and lutein which helps prevent age-related loss of eyesight.

SPINACH, TURMERIC AND LEMON SOUP
Serves 6

This is a lovely coloured soup and very tasty.

4 tbsp olive oil
2 onions, peeled and chopped
900g, 2lb spinach, chopped
rind and juice of 1 lemon
1 tbsp turmeric
1.2 litres, 2pts chicken stock
salt and pepper
6 tbsp natural yoghurt

Cook the onions in the oil in a large saucepan until soft. Add the spinach, lemon rind, juice, turmeric and chicken stock. Season with salt and pepper and bring to the boil. Then simmer for 30 minutes. Cool and purée. Reheat and serve with a spoonful of yoghurt added to each bowl of soup.

CHARD AND CORIANDER SOUP
Serves 6

25g, 1oz butter
2 leeks, chopped
3 potatoes, peeled and chopped
1.2 litres, 2pts vegetable stock
225g, 8oz chard, chopped with stalks removed
2 tbsp coriander, chopped
large pinch salt
3 tbsp crème fraîche

Melt the butter and add the leeks and potatoes. Cook for a few minutes. Add a little stock, and then the chard, coriander and salt. Cook until the chard wilts and then add the remaining stock. Bring to the boil and simmer for about 10 minutes. Liquidise the soup and reheat if necessary. Swirl in the crème fraîche just before serving.

FLORENTINE EGGS
Serves 4

450g, 1lb fresh spinach
4 spring onions, chopped
4 slices ham
4 eggs
2 tbsp single cream

Cook the spinach for a couple of minutes in a covered saucepan so that it wilts. Line 4 gratin dishes with the spinach. Arrange the ham and spring onions on top and crack an egg into the centre of each one. Top each one with a little cream. Place the dishes in a roasting tin half filled with boiling water and bake at gas mark 5, 190°C (375°F) for 20 minutes. Serve with hot rolls.

SPINACH, EGG AND HAM PIE
Serves 6

350g, 12oz shortcrust pastry
1 onion, peeled and sliced
1 clove of garlic, peeled and crushed
2 tbsp olive oil
275g, 10oz spinach
225g, 8oz ham
225g, 8oz mozzarella cheese, sliced
1 red pepper, deseeded and chopped
4 eggs, beaten

Roll the pastry into two rounds, one slightly bigger than the other. Line a greased 20cm, 8in pie dish with the bigger round and keep the other round for the lid. Sauté the onion and garlic in the oil. Cook the spinach for a few minutes in a little water and then drain and chop it before stirring into the onion mixture. Lay slices of ham on the pastry base. Cover with the mozzarella and then the spinach mixture. Add the chopped red pepper. Pour the beaten eggs over the top, reserving a little. Cover with the pastry lid, brush with the reserved egg and cut slits in the pastry. Bake in the oven at gas mark 6, 200°C (400°F) for 35 minutes, or until golden on top.

SPINACH AND BACON QUICHE
Serves 4 – 6

This quiche is popular with the whole family.

225g, 8oz shortcrust pastry
15g, ½oz butter
100g, 4oz streaky bacon, chopped
1 onion, peeled and chopped
3 eggs
150ml, ¼pt single cream
90ml, 3fl oz milk
100g, 4oz spinach, finely chopped
50g, 2oz mature Cheddar cheese, grated

Roll out the pastry and use to line a greased 20cm, 8in flan tin. Prick the base and bake blind in the oven at gas mark 4, 180°C (350°F) for 10 minutes. Melt the butter in a frying pan and add the bacon and onion. Cook until softened. Scatter over the pastry base. Spread the chopped spinach over the bacon and onion. Beat the eggs with the cream and milk and pour over the bacon and spinach. Lastly, scatter the grated cheese over the top and return the quiche to the oven for 30 minutes.

SPINACH SOUFFLÉ
Serves 3 – 4
see photo in colour section

225g, 8oz fresh spinach
50g, 2oz butter
1 tbsp flour
150ml, ¼pt milk
4 eggs, separated
25g, 1oz mature Cheddar cheese, grated

Wash the spinach and cook it with no extra liquid in a saucepan for about 3 minutes. Drain it well and squeeze out any excess moisture. Chop it finely and cook briefly in half the butter. Melt the remaining butter in a saucepan and add the flour. Gradually add the milk and make up a white sauce. Remove from the heat and add the egg yolks. Beat in the grated cheese and then mix in the spinach. Beat the egg whites until stiff and fold these in. Spoon into a soufflé dish and bake in the oven at gas mark 5, 190°C (375°F) for about 25 minutes or until well risen.

SPINACH ROULADE
Serves 3 – 4

675g, 1½lb fresh spinach, washed
4 eggs, separated
pinch of nutmeg

Cheese sauce

40g, 1½oz butter
25g, 1oz flour
300ml, ½pt milk
100g, 4oz mature Cheddar cheese, grated
cayenne pepper

To make the roulade, cook the spinach without any water in a covered saucepan for a few minutes. Drain off any liquid that has formed and chop finely. Mix the egg yolks with the spinach and season with nutmeg. Whisk the egg whites until they form soft peaks. Stir a tablespoon of egg white into the spinach mixture and then fold in the rest in 2 batches. Pour this mixture into a lined, greased Swiss roll tin and bake in the oven at gas mark 6, 200°C (400°F) for 10 minutes. Turn the roulade out onto a clean sheet of greaseproof paper and peel off the lining paper. Make the cheese sauce by melting the butter, stirring in the flour and gradually adding the milk. Stir until smooth and mix in half the grated cheese. Spread some of the cheese sauce over the roulade and roll up carefully. Don't worry if it cracks a little – this is normal. Pour the remaining cheese sauce over the top and sprinkle with the remaining grated cheese and a little cayenne pepper. Return to the oven for 5 minutes so that the cheese melts. Serve immediately.

SPINACH AND RICOTTA PANCAKES
Serves 3 – 4

25g, 1oz butter
1 onion, peeled and sliced
1 clove of garlic, crushed
1 small red pepper, deseeded and sliced
225g, 8oz spinach, chopped
100g, 4oz ricotta
8 pancakes
150ml, ¼pt Passata
50g, 2oz Parmesan, grated

Melt the butter and sauté the onion adding the garlic and red pepper. Mix in the spinach and ricotta and heat gently while you stir everything together. Divide this mixture between the pancakes. Roll up and arrange in a greased ovenproof dish. Pour over the Passata and sprinkle with Parmesan. Finish off in the oven at gas mark 6, 200°C (400°F) for 15 minutes.

TAGLIETELLE WITH SPINACH
AND BLUE CHEESE SAUCE
Serves 4

350g, 12oz taglietelle
225g, 8oz spinach
100g, 4oz blue cheese such as Gorgonzola or Roquefort
90ml, 3fl oz milk
25g, 1oz butter
120ml, 4fl oz double cream
25g, 1oz Parmesan, grated

To make the sauce put the butter, milk and blue cheese into a saucepan and stir together over a low heat until the cheese melts and you have a smooth sauce. Add the cream. Cook the pasta according to the packet instructions and drain. Stir into the cheese sauce and stir in the spinach which will wilt in the hot sauce but retain all its goodness. Serve with parmesan if liked.

171

SPINACH AND MUSHROOM LASAGNE
Serves 2 – 3

450g, 1lb spinach, fresh or frozen
6 – 8 sheets of lasagne
225g, 8oz cream cheese
knob of butter
½ tsp thyme, dried or fresh
½ tsp majoram, dried or fresh
225g, 8oz mushrooms, sliced
25g, 1oz butter
150ml, ¼pt vegetable stock
1 tsp soya sauce
75g, 3oz mature Cheddar cheese, grated

Defrost the spinach if you are using frozen or cook fresh spinach for a few minutes in a very little water until it wilts down. Drain, squeeze out any moisture and chop the spinach finely. Mix in the butter and herbs. When cool mix in the cream cheese. Set aside. Sauté the mushrooms in the butter and then reduce the heat and cook for about 10 minutes in a covered pan to extract as much juice as possible. Add the stock and simmer for another 5 minutes. Add the soya sauce and purée in a food processor. Lay half the spinach mixture in the bottom of a greased loaf tin. Cover with 1 or 2 sheets of lasagne. Use some of the mushroom mixture for the next layer and continue until all the mixtures are used up. Finish with a mushroom or spinach layer and sprinkle over the grated cheese. Bake in the oven at gas mark 5, 190°C (375°F) for 30 minutes.

SPINACH AND TOMATO RICE CAKES
Serves 4 – 6

4 tbsp olive oil
1 onion, peeled and chopped
2 cloves of garlic, peeled and crushed
225g, 8oz risotto rice
600ml, 1pt vegetable stock
1 x 400g, 14oz tin of chopped tomatoes
handful of baby spinach leaves
100g, 4oz Cheddar cheese, grated
plain flour

Heat 2 tablespoons of the oil in a frying pan and fry the onion and garlic gently for 5 minutes. Add the rice and stir to coat in the oil. Pour in the stock and tomatoes and simmer for 25 minutes, stirring occasionally. Remove from the heat and stir in the spinach leaves and half the cheese. Leave until cold and then shape into about 12 round cakes. Roll in the flour and fry in batches in the remaining oil in a frying pan. Sprinkle the remaining cheese on the rice cakes and place under a grill until the cheese is bubbling. Serve immediately.

PANCAKES MADE WITH SPINACH
Makes about 8 pancakes

100g, 4oz plain flour
2 eggs
150ml, ¼pt milk
2 tsp oil + 3 tbsp water
225g, 8oz spinach, finely chopped

Put the flour in a bowl and add the eggs, milk and oil. Beat until smooth. Add the water and stir in the spinach. Heat a little oil in a frying pan and pour in about 2 tablespoons of batter. Cook and toss to brown on both sides.

BABY SPINACH AND BACON SALAD
Serves 4

This is almost a meal in itself.

450g, 1lb baby spinach leaves
1 avocado, halved, peeled and chopped
100g, 4oz streaky unsmoked bacon
2 slices of brown bread for croutons
2 tbsp olive oil
3 hard-boiled eggs, halved
extra olive oil + 1 tbsp balsamic vinegar

Arrange the spinach and avocado in a serving bowl. Fry the bacon in its own fat until crisp and then break into bits. Dice the slices of bread and fry in the olive oil until browned and crisp. Scatter the bacon and croutons over the spinach. Arrange the eggs over the salad. Sprinkle with some olive oil and the balsamic vinegar and serve.

SWISS CHARD AND SMOKED HADDOCK RISOTTO
Serves 4

50g, 2oz butter
1 onion, peeled and chopped
350g, 12oz smoked haddock, deskinned
350g, 12oz risotto rice
150ml, ¼pt white wine
1.2 litres, 2pts water
handful of Swiss chard including stems, chopped
50g, 2oz Parmesan, grated
1 tbsp fresh parsley, chopped

Melt the butter in a frying pan and fry the onion until softened. Add the rice and stir to coat in the butter. Over a low heat gradually add the wine and water, allowing the rice to absorb the liquid before adding more. Add the chard stems when the rice is half cooked. When nearly all the liquid has been absorbed add the chopped chard leaves. At the last minute add the Parmesan and parsley and serve at once.

SWISS CHARD WITH SOURED CREAM
Serve 3 – 4

450g, 1lb Swiss chard, leaves and stems separated
50g, 2oz butter
2 tbsp soured cream
1 tbsp creamed horseradish
salt and pepper

Cut the stems into 2.5cm, 1in slices and steam for a few minutes until tender. Put into a small saucepan with half the butter and over a gentle heat melt the butter and stir in the soured cream and horseradish. Meanwhile steam the leaves until they wilt. Press out any extra moisture, chop and add the remaining butter. Turn into a serving dish and pour the stems and sauce on top.

SWEETCORN

It is thought that maize was first cultivated in Mexico around 7000BC. The Aztecs were keen maize growers. Maize was a staple crop for the North Americans from about 800AD but was not introduced into Europe until the 1500s.

Sweetcorn is a sweet form of maize and it is the yellow varieties that are cultivated for eating. Maize is the third most important cereal in the world and is used for more than 500 by-products. For example the starch extracted after the milling process was used as laundry starch and the inner husks can be used for making cigarette papers. Polenta or cornmeal is made from ground maize. Other products made from maize are corn oil (which incidentally is said to be more effective in lowering cholesterol levels that other polyunsaturated oils) and the seeds from maize provide us with popcorn. Maize is also of course an important animal feed.

Sweetcorn is not that difficult to grow but it does take up a lot of space. It needs a moisture-retentive, free-draining soil to which well-rotted manure has been added a few weeks before planting.It is probably best to sow seeds in pots under cover in late spring, and then thin to leave the strongest seedlings. Plant them out when the danger of all frosts has passed. It is best to plant seedlings in a block with about 16 plants spaced about 30cm, 1ft apart. The reason for this is that sweetcorn is pollinated by wind. The male flowers stand above the top of the plants and shed large amounts of pollen. The female flower is an immature cob with a thin tube hanging from each grain with silk forming at the end. In order for the seeds to develop each strand of silk must receive its own pollen grain. Growing the plants in a block gives them a better chance of pollination.

Growing sweetcorn in this country is slightly risky since it needs a long, warm growing season to do well. Keep the soil moist and water well once the plants begin to flower. Plants may need staking as they are shallow rooted – or you could earth up round the plants to make them more stable. Each plant will only produce one or two cobs. When they are ready the silks will wither and turn dark brown. You can peel back the leaves and test for ripeness by pushing your thumb into a grain. If the liquid runs clear it is unripe. If it is milky, then it is ripe and if it is thick, it is over-ripe. Cobs should be eaten as soon after picking as possible because after 24 hours the sugars in the corn start to turn to starch. If you want to produce popcorn you need to leave the corn on the plants and when the plants die towards the end of September, harvest the cobs on a dry sunny day and leave them to dry outside. When the grains are very dry, rub them from the cobs onto a tray. Store the tray in a warm room for a few weeks by which time the corn should be ready for popping. Heat oil in a saucepan, add the corn, cover and cook until you hear it popping.

Sweetcorn is high in fibre and contains vitamin C and A. It is also a good source of potassium.

SPICY SWEETCORN AND POTATO
Serves 4

1 small red onion, peeled and sliced
1 tbsp olive oil
1 tsp cumin seeds
½ tsp hot paprika
450g, 1lb new potatoes, cooked and diced
sweetcorn from 6 cobs or 1 x 325g, 12oz can
juice of ½ a lemon
pinch of garam masala
2 tbsp fresh chives, chopped

Sauté the onion in the olive oil until soft. Add the cumin seeds and fry for a minute. Add the paprika, potatoes and sweetcorn. Then stir in the lemon juice and add the garam masala. Take off the heat and sprinkle with the chives before serving.

SWEETCORN FRITTERS
Serves 4

100g, 4oz self-raising flour
1 egg
150ml, ¼pt milk
1 tsp olive oil
50g, 2oz Cheddar cheese, grated
225g, 8oz sweetcorn, either fresh from the cob or tinned
oil for frying

Make the batter by combining the flour, egg, milk and olive oil. You can whiz these up in the food processor. Stir in the cheese and sweetcorn. Heat some oil in a large frying pan and drop spoonfuls of the batter into the pan. Fry until brown on both sides and serve.

RICH SWEETCORN AND PARSNIP FLAN
Serves 3 – 4

Cream cheese pastry

75g, 3oz cream cheese
75g, 3oz butter
175g, 6oz flour
2 tsp baking powder
generous pinch of chilli powder

1 onion, peeled and sliced
2 parsnips, peeled, cooked and mashed
175g, 6oz sweetcorn
3 eggs
150ml, ¼pt milk
75g, 3oz mature Cheddar cheese, grated
2 tomatoes, sliced

Put the cream cheese and butter in a food processor and whiz to mix together. Then add the flour, baking powder and pinch of chilli powder. Whiz again to form a dough. Take the dough out and shape into a ball, then chill in the fridge for about 20 minutes. Roll out and use the pastry to line a greased 20cm, 8in flan dish. Bake blind for 10 minutes in the oven at gas mark 4, 180°C (350°F). Gently fry the onion in the olive oil until soft. Mix in the parsnip and sweetcorn. Beat the eggs with the milk. Add to the vegetable mixture and stir over a low heat until the mixture is close to setting. Pour onto the pastry base and top with the cheese and slices of tomatoes. Cook in the oven for a further 20 minutes.

SWEETCORN AND CARROT CRUMBLE
Serves 4

2 large carrots, peeled and sliced
15g, ½oz butter
2 tsp clear honey
3 tbsp vegetable stock
sweetcorn from 6 cobs or 1 x 325g, 12oz can
1 tbsp fresh parsley, chopped

Crumble
100g, 4oz wholemeal flour
50g, 2oz margarine
25g, 1oz brown breadcrumbs
50g, 2oz Cheddar cheese, grated

Cook the carrots for a few minutes and then dice them up. Stir in the butter, honey and stock. Mix with the sweetcorn and transfer to a baking dish. Sprinkle on the parsley. To make the crumble rub the margarine into the flour and stir in the breadcrumbs and cheese. Sprinkle over the vegetables and cook in the oven at gas mark 5, 190°C (375°F) until the crumble looks brown and crisp.

SWEETCORN AND TOMATO BAKE
Serves 4

This dish is quite filling and can be served as a main vegetarian dish with French bread or as a side dish with plainly cooked meat or fish.

3 tbsp olive oil
1 clove of garlic, peeled and crushed
225g, 8oz tomatoes, chopped
1 green pepper, deseeded and chopped
sweetcorn from 6 cobs or 1 x 325g, 12oz can
2 tbsp peanuts, unsalted
4 tbsp double cream
2 eggs, separated

Heat the oil in a frying pan and add the garlic, tomatoes and pepper. Fry for several minutes and then add the sweetcorn including the water in the can. Cook for another 5 minutes and then transfer to an ovenproof dish and add the peanuts. Mix the cream with the egg yolks and stir into the vegetables. Whisk the egg whites until they are stiff and fold them in with a metal spoon. Cook in the oven at gas mark 6, 200°C (400°F) for about 20 minutes or until golden.

TOMATOES

The tomato originated in Mexico in Central America and like the potato was brought to Europe by Spanish Conquistadors. It was introduced into Europe through Italy in the 1500s. At first it was thought to be poisonous and was grown as an ornamental plant. The tomato comes from the same family as the potato and so is also related to the Deadly Nightshade. Like the potato the tomato has poisonous leaves. First known in Europe as 'pomme d'amour' – love apple, (which in itself must have derived from the Italian word 'pomodoro' – golden apple) the first tomatoes seen in Europe were small and yellow. The word tomato comes from the Mexican 'tomatl'.

There are so many different varieties of tomatoes on the market that I am not going to describe them all here. I usually grow Gardener's Delight (a popular variety of cherry tomatoes) in grow bags and they can be very successful providing we have a long, warm, sunny summer. The season is too short to grow tomatoes from seeds sown in situ. Outdoor tomatoes are always grown from plants and are readily available from Garden Centres in late spring. They can be raised from seeds sown in a heated propagator at the beginning of March. Plants can be planted outside once the first flowering truss can be seen and once all risk of frost has passed, usually at the end of May. If using grow bags or pots you must keep the tomato plants well watered and it is a good idea to use a bio tomato feed every two weeks. Tomatoes should be ripening up and ready for picking from mid August through September.

Tomatoes contain lycopene, an antioxidant phytochemical which helps prevent heart disease and some cancers. Lycopene is actually more effective in cooked or canned tomatoes. So tomato purée, juice and ketchup are all very beneficial. Tomatoes also contain beta-carotene, Vitamins C and E and potassium.

Like onions, tomatoes are used in a multitude of dishes. Here I have given you some ideas for when you have a glut.

TOMATO AND BASIL SOUP
Serves 6

2 tbsp olive oil
1 onion, peeled and chopped
3 tbsp flour
1.2 litres, 2pts vegetable stock
2 tbsp tomato purée
1 tbsp fresh basil, chopped
1kg, 2.2lb tomatoes
salt and pepper
150ml, ¼pt single cream

Heat the oil in a saucepan and add the onions. Cook until browned and then add the flour. Gradually add the stock over a low heat and stir until thick and smooth. Stir in the tomato purée, basil, tomatoes and seasoning. Cover and simmer for 30 minutes. Sieve or purée in a blender, return to the saucepan to reheat and pour into bowls, swirling a little cream over each portion.

BAKED EGGS IN TOMATOES
Serves 4

4 large, firm beef tomatoes
6 tbsp wholemeal breadcrumbs
1 tbsp fresh chives + 1 tbsp fresh parsley, chopped
2 tbsp Parmesan cheese, grated
4 eggs

Cut the tops off the tomatoes and discard. Scoop out the centres but don't go too near the edges. Chop up and mix with 2 tablespoons of the breadcrumbs and the herbs. Pack some of the mixture back into each tomato and break an egg into each cavity. Top with the rest of the breadcrumbs mixed with the Parmesan. Bake in the oven at gas mark 4, 180°C (350°F) for about 30 minutes or until the tomatoes are soft.

TOMATO CHARLOTTE
Serves 4

12 thin slices brown bread
75g, 3oz butter
1kg, 2.2lb tomatoes, blanched, skinned and sliced
salt and pepper
1 tsp sugar
1 tsp basil, fresh or dried
50g, 2oz mature Cheddar cheese, grated

Butter all the slices of bread on one side and cut each slice into three. Line a pie dish with the bread, butter side down. Put in a layer of tomatoes and season with salt, pepper, sugar and basil. Cover with a layer of bread, then add the remaining tomatoes, seasoning them and top with the remaining bread. Sprinkle on the cheese and cook in the oven at gas mark 4, 180°C (350°F) for 30 minutes. The bread should be crisp round the edges. Serve hot with any green veg or a salad.

CARAMELISED, ROASTED TOMATOES
Serves 3 – 4

450g, 1lb vine or cherry tomatoes
1 tbsp brown sugar
2 tbsp extra virgin olive oil
sprinkling of balsamic vinegar

Halve the tomatoes, sprinkle with the brown sugar and fry in the oil in a large frying pan for a couple of minutes. Sprinkle with balsamic vinegar and finish off in the oven at gas mark 5, 190°C (375°F) for 10 minutes.

TOMATO AND PUY LENTIL SALAD
Serves 3 – 4

300ml, ½pt vegetable stock
225g, 8oz puy lentils
2 tbsp olive oil
4 spring onions, chopped
4 tomatoes, chopped
1 yellow pepper, deseeded and chopped
sprinkling of balsamic vinegar
1 tbsp fresh parsley, chopped

Bring the stock to the boil in a saucepan and add the lentils. Simmer in the stock for 20 minutes. In the meantime heat the oil in a frying pan and add the spring onion, tomatoes and pepper – fry for several minutes until browned. Drain the lentils and transfer to a warm serving dish. Cover with the fried vegetables. Sprinkle with balsamic vinegar and add the parsley.

TOMATO AND PINEAPPLE RELISH
Makes approx 1.8kg, 4lb

This has a sweet and sour flavour and goes well with cold meats or cheese.

1 tbsp olive oil
2 onions, peeled and chopped
4 garlic cloves, peeled and chopped
2kg, 4¼lb tomatoes
350g, 12oz sugar
1 tbsp salt
½ tbsp paprika
450g, 1lb tin of pineapple pieces
600ml, 1pt white wine vinegar

Heat the oil in a large pan and cook the onions and garlic for a few minutes until softened. Add all the other ingredients, bring to the boil and then simmer for about 1 hour, stirring every so often, by which time the relish should be thick. Spoon into sterilized jars and seal. This relish should keep for a few months.

GREEN TOMATO CHUTNEY
Makes approx 2.5kg, 6lb

450g, 1lb cooking apples, peeled, cored and chopped
225g, 8oz onions, skinned and chopped
1.4kg, 3lb green tomatoes, sliced
225g, 8oz sultanas
225g, 8oz demerara sugar
2 tsp salt
450ml, ¾pt malt vinegar
2.5cm, 1in piece of root ginger, grated
½ tsp cayenne pepper
1 tsp mustard powder

Put all the ingredients in a preserving pan. Bring to the boil, reduce the heat and simmer gently for about 2 hours, stirring occasionally, until the ingredients are tender and reduced to a thick consistency. Spoon the chutney into jars and seal.

TURNIPS AND SWEDES

Turnips were grown by the Greeks and Romans and it was probably the Romans who brought them to Britain. They are a useful crop to grow as you can eat the turnip tops (leaves), cooking them like cabbage. The swede is similar to the turnip and originated, not surprisingly, in Sweden arriving in Britain around 1781. The swede is a hybrid between a turnip and a cabbage and in times of famine it was a useful food for poorer people. It differs from the turnip in that it is larger, hardier, stores better and has a milder taste although it does take longer to grow. Nowadays there are some excellent disease-resistant varieties available and it makes a good winter vegetable to use along with Brussels sprouts.

Turnips and swedes will grow in almost any soil. Turnip seeds should be sown any time between April and the end of June in rows 30cm, 12in apart. Thin the seedlings to 10cm, 4in apart. Turnips mature rapidly so you should be harvesting young turnips from June through into the autumn for maincrop turnips. Young turnips have a delicate flavour with purple or green tinged skin. Maincrop turnips have thicker skins and coarse flesh. Swedes are a winter crop and need to be sown in early June. You should thin the seedlings to about 23cm, 9in apart as spacing is important to obtain decent-sized roots - they should be about the size of a grapefruit - you should be able to harvest them from October to December. They store well but you need to twist the leaves off leave the roots on and store in boxes of sand in a cool shed.

Turnips have a very high water content of around 90% so are low in calories. Nutritionally swedes and turnips supply some vitamin C and swedes supply some niacin (vitamin B).

TURNIPS PAYSANNE
Serves 4

450g, 1lb young turnips, scrubbed or peeled
1 tbsp sunflower oil
1 onion, peeled and chopped

4 rashers unsmoked bacon, chopped
4 tbsp brown breadcrumbs +1 tbsp chopped parsley

Cook the turnips in boiling salted water until tender. Fry the onion in the oil and add the bacon. Fry until crisp and then add the turnips and cook for a few minutes. Transfer to a serving dish. Add the breadcrumbs to the frying pan and fry until crisp. Mix with the parsley and scatter over the turnips.

TURNIP AND WATERCRESS PURÉE
Serves 4 – 6

450g, 1lb turnips, peeled and diced
225g, 8oz potatoes, peeled and chopped
1 bunch of watercress
salt and pepper

Put the turnips and potatoes in a saucepan with water to cover and bring to the boil. Simmer for 25 minutes and then add the watercress and simmer for one more minute. Drain, reserving some of the water. Purée the vegetables in a blender or processor and add a little of the cooking water and a knob of butter. Add salt and pepper and turn into a serving dish.

SWEDE AND APPLE PURÉE
Serves 6

900g, 2lb swedes, peeled and sliced
50g, 2oz butter
350g, 12oz cooking apples, peeled, cored and sliced
salt, pepper + a pinch of nutmeg
1 tsp sugar
1 tbsp double cream (optional)

Boil the swedes in salted water until soft, then drain and mash them with the butter until smooth. Cook the apples in a little water until tender and stir into the swede purée. Add salt, pepper, nutmeg and sugar. A spoonful of double cream may also be added.

My Gardening Calendar

This is based on what I grow for the family at the moment to produce a succession of vegetables all year round - I tend to stick to vegetables that are popular with the children.

	Sowing	Harvesting
January/ February	Under the cloche: varieties of cut-and-come-again salad leaves; rocket; mustard leaves, spinach. Broad beans; shallots; Jerusalem artichokes.	Curly kale; radicchio; Brussels sprouts; early purple sprouting broccoli.
March	Potatoes; onion sets; beetroot; radishes; parsnips; spinach.	Purple sprouting broccoli; curly kale.
April	Mangetout; carrots; more salad leaves; Swiss chard; more parsnips (if not successful in March).	Any remaining broccoli; salad leaves or spinach that has overwintered; early broad beans.
May	More carrots. Plant out Brassica seedlings such as cauliflower, broccoli and Brussels sprouts.	Salad leaves; rocket; spinach; radishes.
June	French and Runner beans; kale; seedlings for courgettes, tomatoes, squash, outdoor cucumbers.	Broad beans; mangetout and sugar snap peas (usually at end of June - popular with the children); early potatoes.
July	Final crop of beetroot; kale, radicchio and endive.	Shallots; salad leaves; potatoes; carrots.
August/ September	For autumn and overwintering: Lettuces such as Rouge d'Hiver, Rougette du Midi; Spinach such as Giant Winter and Perpetual Spinach; mustard leaves.	French and runner beans; carrots; lettuce; courgettes, cucumbers and tomatoes; pumpkins and squashes; carrots; beetroot; Swiss chard.
October/ November/ December	Broad beans (Super Aquadulce) for an early crop in the Spring.	Parsnips after first frosts; kale; Swiss chard; radicchio and endive; Jerusalem artichokes.

Index

A

Apple 46, 49, 56, 63, 65, 70, 71, 81, 83-85, 121, 124, 127, 136, 181, 185, 187
Artichoke 96 - 99
Artichoke & Potato Croquettes 98
Artichokes au Gratin 99
Artichokes with Tomato Sauce 99
Asparagus 5 - 9, 130
Asparagus with Cream Cheese 8
Aubergine 11, 12, 13, 94
Aubergine Dip 10
Aubergines Parmigiana 13
Avocado 70, 71, 112, 174

B

Baby Spinach & Bacon Salad 174
Bacon, Egg & Potato Bake 149
Bacon Potato Cakes 148
Bacon Steaks with Cucumber & Apple Sauce 84
Baked Eggs in Tomatoes 182
Baked Layered Potatoes 147
Beef 39, 75, 135, 140
Beetroot 14 - 19, 164
Beetroot & Chocolate Cake 18
Beetroot & Tuna Quiche 17
Beetroot, Spinach & Mackerel Salad 17
Beetroot & Tomato Soup 16
Beetroot Baked in Cream & Lemon 16
Beetroot Relish 19
Beetroot Salad 19
Borlotti Bean & Aubergine Dip 94
Borlotti Bean &Tuna Pasta Salad 94
Borlotti Beans 89, 90, 94
Braised Celery with Pine Nuts 64
Braised Endive 67

Braised Fennel 87
Braised Lettuce with Carrots 114
Broad Bean & Ham Salad 22
Broad Bean & Mint Soup 21
Broad Bean Omelette 23
Broad Beans 8, 9, 20 - 23
Broad Beans with Cream & Bacon 22
Broccoli 24 - 31, 54
Broccoli in Curried Lemon Mayonnaise 29
Broccoli Muffins 31
Broccoli with Anchovy & Garlic 28
Broccoli with Egg & Mushroom 27
Brussel Sprouts With Hazelnuts & Bacon 33
Brussels Sprout Purée 36
Brussels Sprout Soup 34
Brussels Sprouts 32 - 36, 97, 101, 102, 181, 186
Bubble & Squeak 42
Butternut Squash Risotto with Rocket 156

C

Cabbage 24, 37- 42, 165,181
Cabbage Steamed in the Wok 41
Caesar Salad 114
Cake 18, 49, 51, 79, 148, 152, 158
Cannelloni Stuffed with Tuna & Red Peppers 141
Caramelised Roasted Tomatoes 183
Carrot & Apple Coleslaw 46
Carrot & Apple Tart 49
Carrot & Kale with Poppy Seeds 49
Carrot & Lentil Soup 45
Carrot & Parsnip Fritters 48
Carrot Cake 44, 51
Carrot, Cheese & Tarragon Soufflé 46
Carrot Marmalade 53
Carrot Muffins 50
Carrot, Tomato & Lemon Soup 45
Carrots 35, 43 - 50, 53, 57, 103, 128, 138, 179
Cauliflower 54 - 61

189

Cauliflower Florets with Olive Oil &
    Lemon Dressing 56
Cauliflower Salad 56
Celeriac 62, 64, 65
Celeriac & Potato Purée 64
Celeriac Remoulade 65
Celeriac Salad 64
Celery 62, 63, 64
Char Grilled Asparagus with
    Breadcrumb Topping 7
Chard 104, 164, 166, 174, 175
Cheesy Broccoli Soup 25
Cheesy Cauliflower Soup 55
Cheesy Duchess Potatoes 148
Cheesy Parsnip & Tomato Bake 126
Chicken, Carrot & Lemon Pie 47
Chicory 66, 68, 69, 70
Chicory au Gratin 69
Chicory, Avocado & Tomato Salad 70
Chicory in Mustard Sauce 68
Chocolate Cake 18, 152
Colcannon with Kale 101
Courgette 72 -77, 79,
    80, 153, 155, 157
Courgette and Bacon Bake 76
Courgette & Goat's Cheese Flan 76
Courgette Moussaka 75
Creamed Chicken with Asparagus 7
Creamed Lettuce & Cucumber Soup
    113
Creamy Broad Beans with Sweet
    Corn 23
Creamy Cabbage Bake 42
Crisp Onion Rings 120
Crispy Potato Skins 146
Cucumber 82 - 85, 113, 163
Cucumber Relish 85
Cucumber with Egg & Lemon Sauce
    85
Curly Kale Soup 101
Curried Cauliflower 58
Curried Parsnip & Apple Soup 124

D

Date and Chocolate Spread 150

E

Endive 66, 67
Endive, Egg And Anchovy Salad 67

F

Fennel 64, 65, 86, 87, 88
Fennel, Potato & Anchovy Salad 87
Florence Fennel 86 *see Fennel*
Florentine Eggs 166
French Bean Purée 92
French Beans 89 - 93
French Beans with Pears 93
French Style Creamy Peas & Lettuce
    133
Fritters 48, 60, 73, 156, 178

G

Glazed Carrots with Hazelnuts 48
Glazed Parsnips 126
Green Pepper 140, 180
Green Tomato Chutney 185

H

Hazelnuts 33, 48, 97, 136
Hot Cauliflower & Carrot Salad 57
Hot Potato Salad 150

J

Jerusalem Artichokes 96 *see
Artichokes*

K

Kale 49, 100 - 103
Kale & Carrot au Gratin 103

L

Leek 104 - 109, 112, 166
Leek & Goat's Cheese Tortilla 108

Leek & Mushroom Croustade 109
Leek & Potato Soup 105
Leek & Tomato Tart 106
Leek Purée 105
Lentils 45, 115, 154, 184
Lentil, Rocket & Sorrel Tart 115
Lettuce 56, 110 - 114, 133
Lettuce & Avocado Soup 112

M

Mackerel 17
Mangetout 129, 130, 136-138, 162
Mangetout & Apple Salad With
    Toasted Hazelnuts 136
Mangetout & Bacon Salad 137
Marrow & Apple Chutney 81
Marrow & Tomato Bake 78
Marrows 72, 78, 153
Mediterranean Fish & Fennel
    Casserole 88
Moussaka 12
Muffins 31, 50, 159
Mushroom
    27, 47, 60, 88, 93, 109, 141, 172

O

Omelette 23, 34
Onion 9, 115 - 120, 148, 181
Onion & Apple Chutney 121
Onion Bhajis 120
Onion Tart 119
Oriental-style Stir Fried Kale 102

P

Pancakes made with Spinach 173
Parsnip 48, 122 - 128, 163, 179
Parsnip & Carrot Purée 128
Parsnip & Tomato Soup 125
Parsnip, Carrot & Apple Roast 127
Parsnip Croquettes 127
Parsnip, Date & Ginger Loaf 123, 128
Pasta With Broccoli, Tuna & Ancho-
    vies 26

Pasta with Tuna & Mangetout 137
Pea & Beef Meatballs 135
Pea, Lemon & Sorrel Soup 131
Pea, Pear & Mint Soup 132
Pea Purée with Noodles & Bacon 135
Pea Tarts 133
Peapod Soup 131
Peas 112, 129 - 135, 156
Peppers 139 - 143
Pine Nuts 28, 29, 64
Potato 21, 42, 64, 87, 98, 101, 105,
    144 -149, 151 - 152, 177, 181, 188
Potato Biscuits 151
Potato Bread 151
Potato Drop Scones 159
Potato Pancakes 147
Potatoes in Spicy Tomato Sauce 149
Prawn, Apple & Radicchio Salad 70
Pumpkin 153 - 155, 158 -160
Pumpkin & Lemon Soup 155
Pumpkin & Pecan Muffins 159
Pumpkin Pie 160
Pumpkin Scones 159
Purple Sprouting Broccoli with Tomato
    Cream 30
Purple Sprouting Broccoli with Walnut
    Butter 30

R

Radicchio 66, 70, 71
Radish 161 - 163
Radish, Cottage Cheese & Cucumber
    Salad 163
Radish Soup 162
Ratatouille 11
Red Onion Marmalade 121
Red Pepper 34, 80, 92, 139, 142, 143,
    167, 171
Red Pepper, Spinach & Tomato Risotto
    142
Rich Sweetcorn & Parsnip Flan 178
Risi E Bisi 134
Risotto 8, 9, 142, 156, 173,174
Roasted Radishes & Root Vegetables 163

Roasted Squash with Courgette &
    Tomato 155
Rocket 111, 115, 142, 156
Rocket Salsa 115
Runner Beans 89, 90, 94, 95
Runner Beans a la Grecque 94
Runner Beans au Gratin 95

S

Salad 17, 19, 22, 37, 56, 63 - 64
67, 70-71, 87, 110, 111, 114,
117, 137, 150, 163, 174, 184
Salade Nicoise 91
Sautéed French Beans with Red
    Pepper 92
Sautéed Radishes & Mangetout 162
Savoury Squash Bake 157
Savoy Cabbage 37, 41
Shallots 116
Soup 6, 15, 16, 21, 25, 34, 45,
55, 83, 97, 98, 101, 105, 112, 113, 119, 124,
125, 130 - 32, 154, 155, 162,
165, 166, 182
Spicy Sweetcorn & Potato 177
Spinach 17, 112, 142, 164 - 174
Spinach & Bacon Quiche 168
Spinach & Mushroom Lasagne 172
Spinach & Ricotta Pancakes 171
Spinach & Tomato Rice Cakes 173
Spinach, Egg & Ham Pie 167
Spinach Roulade 170
Spinach Soufflé 169
Sprout Omelette 34
Sprouts & Carrots in Tomato Cream
    Sauce 35
Sprouts with Chestnuts 36
Sprouts with Poppy Seeds & Lemon
    35
Squash 97, 98, 153 - 157
Squash & Courgette Rosti 157
Squash & Pea Fritters 156
Sticky Toffee Pudding with Carrots 52
Stir Fried Cabbage with Sesame Seeds
    40

Stir Fried Cabbage with Yoghurt &
    Horseradish 40
Stir Fried Kale with Sprouts 102
Stuffed Cabbage Leaves 39
Stuffed Pepper Soufflés 143
Stuffed Peppers 140
Sugar Snap Peas 137, 162
Swede 186, 187
Swede And Apple Purée 187
Sweet & Sour Cabbage 41
Sweet Pepper And Herb Flan 142
Sweetcorn 23 , 71, 176 - 180
Sweetcorn & Carrot Crumble 179
Sweetcorn & Tomato Bake 180
Sweetcorn Fritters 178
Swiss Chard & Smoked Haddock
    Risotto 174
Swiss Chard with Soured Cream 175

T

Taglietelle with Spinach & Blue
    Cheese Sauce 171
Toasted Cheese & Onion Soup 119
Tomato
    30, 70, 71, 77, 78, 80, 88, 91, 95,
106, 109, 121, 125, 126, 142, 143,
155, 180 - 185
Tomato & Basil Soup 182
Tomato & Pineapple Relish 184
Tomato & Puy Lentil Salad 184
Tomato Charlotte 183
Tuna 17, 26, 91, 94, 107, 137, 141
Turkey and Mangetout Stir Fry 138
Turkey Meatballs With Leeks 108
Turnip 186, 188
Turnip & Watercress Purée 187
Turnips Paysanne 186

W

Waldorf Salad 63
Walnuts 30, 63, 70, 74, 75, 79
Wholemeal Pumpkin & Lemon Cake
    158